W9-DCI-201

Praise for
Opening to You by Norman Fischer

"Astonishing . . . Reading these alone will make the
heart soar . . . [Fischers's] desire, pure and simple,
was to bring clarity for today's spiritual seeker. These
inspired renditions succeed admirably and invite all
to partake."
    —*NAPRA Review*

"Norman's beautiful and poetic new versions of the
timeless Psalms help awaken us from mindless
distraction and enter into the mysterious music of
sacred living."
    —Lama Surya Das, author of *Awakening the
    Buddha Within*

"The beauty in these poems is healing; it can make us
whole as only beauty can. May it serve to help people
join with one another, and ourselves to join with
ourselves. This is a crucial time for these wondrous
songs to reach us."
    —Daniel Ladinsky, translator of *The Gift* by Hafiz

ABOUT THE AUTHOR

Norman Fischer is a renowned Zen priest, teacher, poet, and former co-abbot of the San Francisco Zen Center and a featured contributor to *Benedict's Dharma*. As the founder of the Everyday Zen Foundation (www.EverydayZen.org), he organizes Zen lectures and retreats as well as Jewish meditation classes and is actively involved in interfaith dialogue. He lives in Muir Beach, California.

OPENING

TO

YOU

Zen-Inspired

Translations

of the

Psalms

PENGUIN
COMPASS

PENGUIN COMPASS
Published by the Penguin Group
Penguin Putnam Inc., 375 Hudson Street,
New York. New York 10014, U.S.A.
Penguin Books Ltd. 80 Strand, London WC2R 0RL, England
Penguin Books Australia Ltd. 250 Camberwell Road,
Camberwell, Victoria 3124, Australia
Penguin Books Canada Ltd, 10 Alcorn Avenue,
Toronto, Ontario, Canada M4V 3B2
Penguin Books India (P) Ltd, 11 Community Centre,
Panchsheel Park, New Delhi – 110 017, India
Penguin Books (N.Z.) Ltd, Cnr Rosedale and Airborne Roads,
Albany, Auckland, New Zealand
Penguin Books (South Africa) (Pty) Ltd, 24 Sturdee Avenue,
Rosebank, Johannesburg 2196, South Africa

Penguin Books Ltd, Registered Offices:
Harmondsworth, Middlesex, England

First published in the United States of America by Viking Compass,
a member of Penguin Putnam Inc. 2002
Published in Penguin Compass 2003

1   3   5   7   9   10   8   6   4   2

Copyright © Norman Fisher, 2002
All rights reserved

THE LIBRARY OF CONGRESS HAS CATALOGED
THE HARDCOVER EDITION AS FOLLOWS:
Fischer, Norman.
Opening to you : Zen-inspired translations of the Psalms / Norman Fisher.
p.   cm.
ISBN 0-670-03061-9 (hc)
ISBN 0 14 21.9613 4 (pbk)
1. Bible. O.T. Psalms—Paraphrases, English.   I. Title.
BS1440 .F54 2001
223'.205209—dc21   2001045437

Set in Filosofia
Designed by Francesca Belanger

This book is in memory of my parents

Sidney and Lenora Fischer

and my grandmother

Fannie Lustig

bound up in the bonds of life

ACKNOWLEDGMENTS

Returning to my roots, to the Psalms, has been an extraordinary and unexpected journey for me, a journey that is only just beginning. I hope there will be time left to continue for a while. There are many people to thank. The hundreds of Buddhist, Christian, Jewish, and other spiritual friends who listened to these Psalms and encouraged me to continue to work with them—especially the students at Makor Or, the Jewish meditation center in San Francisco. The Brothers of Gethsemani and New Camaldoli, for their chanting and for their faith. Brother David Steindl-Rast and Father Laurence Freeman for their friendship and clear vision. My Buddhist teachers and dear friends Jack Kornfield and Sylvia Boorstein, who show me that Buddhism isn't only Buddhism if it is truly Buddhism. Rabbi Gabriel Maza, whose love of God, truth, and questioning has been the inspiration for my life. Rabbi David Whyte, for welcoming me graciously back into the fold when I didn't think anyone would. My closest friend Rabbi Alan Lew, with whom I have walked the path, side by side, for thirty years and more. And my wife, Kathie, and sons, Aron and Noah, for powerful love I have never deserved and did not think possible. Finally I want to thank my editor, Janet Goldstein, for her thoroughness and for her faithfulness to this project, and my agent, Michael Katz, for his persistence and friendship.

CONTENTS

INTRODUCTION

Some years ago I stayed for a week with the Trappist monks of Gethsemani Abbey, Thomas Merton's monastery in the rolling hills of Kentucky. There I encountered for the first time the Christian monastic practice of choir, which consists, for the most part, of daily recitation of the Psalms. Although I had grown up chanting the Psalms in Hebrew (a language I can pronounce but not comprehend), it was at Gethsemani that I first paid attention to what these texts were saying.

There are many uplifting, inspiring, and soaring verses in the Psalms. (Who isn't moved to remember "I will fear no evil, for thou art with me, thy rod and thy staff they comfort me" or "Let everything that breathes praise the Lord!"?) But the passages that caught my ear during those early-morning and evening hours in that Kentucky summer were not those. I was astonished at the violence, passion, and bitterness that were expressed ("Let burning coals fall upon them: let them be cast into the fire; into deep pits, that they rise not up again," cries the speaker in Psalm 140). For me, whose lifelong spiritual practice has been silent Zen sitting meditation, it seemed almost impossible to believe that intoning these disturbing and distancing words could be the basis for a satisfying religious practice. In all innocence I asked the monks about this and received many cogent and impassioned responses: that the anger and violence in the Psalms were human emotions that could find healing through expression; that these things are part of our human life and must not be left out of religious contemplation; that the suffering the Psalms express is holy suffering, and to enter into it is to become close to God; and much more. All of it made some sense to me, but I wasn't really satisfied. Nor could I dismiss the Psalms as irrelevant. I saw that these good brothers of Gethsemani were true treaders of the path, sincere practitioners, possessed of wisdom and knowledge. If the Psalms had meaning for them, clearly I was missing something. I felt I had to investigate for myself. These selected versions of the Psalms are the results of that investigation.

Since I am a poet and a religious practitioner, not a Hebraist, my work with the Psalms rests largely on the work of translators. In that sense they are "versions" rather than translations, perhaps as much original English-language poems as faithful replicas of the Hebrew text. On the other hand, it may be that all translations, especially the best, are versions. It may even be that all poems are only tentative versions of something so intimate it can never be written down. While I have certainly taken liberties of interpretation (otherwise, what is the point?), I have only very seldom added anything and have never subtracted anything. So I do think that these poems are more or less the Psalms as they have come down to us. My effort has been to bring out their latent meanings, rather than to create new meanings.

I decided against rendering the entire psaltery (150 psalms), first, because the Psalms are not all equally interesting or powerful, and there is much repetition, and second, because I thought that too many poems at once would blunt the reader's attention. In a way I am sorry not to have done them all, but also happy, because now I have that as a bright possibility. I have selected 93 poems for this volume, making 173 pages, already quite a lot. I made my selections according to what caught my interest (although I often found that what seemed uninteresting at first became interesting once I had plunged in) and also taking suggestions from many friends and from reading. I tried not to avoid selecting psalms with difficult or even terrible passages.

I call them "Zen-inspired" because I approach them the only way I can: as a Zen practitioner and teacher, with a Zen eye. But I have not tried to rewrite the Psalms as Zen philosophy. Quite the opposite. My intention has been to learn from them, to expand my own understanding under their influence. Nevertheless, although my way of life and understanding have been thoroughly saturated by Zen, I am still a Westerner, so I have found in the Psalms a very familiar music that seems to express my own approach to enlightenment: the passionate, prickly, and lively noise that naturally seems to rise from the silent depths of my own heart.

I do not think I am unusual. Western Buddhists are Buddhists, yes, but they are also Westerners. This makes a big difference. It is why Buddhism in the West is and will continue to be very different from what it has been in Asia. No matter how much Westerners try to immerse themselves in the Buddhism presented to them by their Asian teachers (and expressed in the Asian texts), they will always see it colored by Western concepts and views and by a Western feeling for life. You could view this as a problem, a distortion of real Buddhism, and I know that many Asian Buddhist teachers think that Westerners just don't "get" Buddhism and that it will take several generations for them to get it. While this is a reasonable way to look at it, I prefer to see the problem as an advantage and to view the inevitable mixing of Western and Asian Buddhist perspectives as something fresh and inspired, rather than as somehow incorrect.

I have seen in myself and in my students just how deeply the Western feeling goes. It is simply not to be denied, not to be covered with a veneer of Buddhism. There has been much written of and discussed about this in relation to Western psychology, and in many ways the Western Buddhist movement has been thoroughly, probably for good and for ill, psychologized. But I am sure our Westernness goes deeper than the personal. Our whole sense of what we think of as human, what we think of as the world, and how we are to stand in the world is thoroughly Western, thoroughly Judeo-Christian. Certainly Buddhism will have a powerful effect on these deeply held views if we practice it for a lifetime; for many people the change has already happened. But even so, even as thorough Buddhists, we shall continue to stand on Western ground and continue to hold, in the depths of our hearts, some Judeo-Christian sensibility.

Once at a Jewish-Buddhist retreat he and I were leading at San Francisco Zen Center's remote mountain monastery, called Tassajara, my old friend and colleague Rabbi Alan Lew was asked to make the odious comparison: strengths and weaknesses, Judaism versus Buddhism. He said that the strength of Buddhism is that it is clear and useful and will help your life. Judaism, on the other hand, doesn't make sense, and that is exactly its strength. Just like us, he said. We don't make sense. The weakness of Buddhism, he said, is precisely that it makes too much sense.

Buddhism *does* make sense. It is full of practical advice on how to work with anger, jealousy, confusion, and other painful emotional states, sound advice that supports in many ways the psychological and spiritual preconceptions that many of us hold. But the trouble is, our irrational and sometimes conflicted Western selves that persist somehow, despite all our good Buddhist practice, waylay us now and then with deeply held emotions like longing, sorrow, loss, loneliness, soul confusion. We find there is still sometimes a need to call out, to sing, to shout, to be heard, to be answered. These passions deeply persist even though our hearts are settled. All this is the territory of the Psalms.

The Psalms are a fundamental text of Western Judeo-Christian spirituality, perhaps the most fundamental. They are chanted daily in Christian and Jewish services, and they contain all the theology of the Old and the New Testaments. For three thousand years Western peoples have been contemplating these poems, resonating emotionally their deepest feeling for life through them.

Buddhism begins with suffering and the end of suffering and the path toward the ending of suffering. This is essential and useful for everyone, not just Buddhists. But this approach can easily lead to a grave spiritual error, the notion that suffering is something to be avoided, prevented, escaped, bypassed. I have seen many Western Buddhist students suffer a great deal because of this natural error, thinking and believing they could go beyond or had gone beyond their suffering, only to find that it was there all along, underneath their seeming calmness and insight, and that because they had not seen and accepted it, they allowed it to grow far worse.

The Psalms make it clear that suffering is not to be escaped or bypassed. Much to the contrary, suffering returns again and again, a path in itself, and through the very suffering and the admission of suffering, the letting go into suffering and the calling out from it, mercy and peace can come (this is most poignantly expressed, of course, in the example of Jesus).

There is a crucial corollary to this point: If suffering is a path, then those who suffer are to be honored. A key theme of the Psalms, and therefore of Judaism and Christianity, is the nobility of the oppressed and the necessity of justice and righteousness, that the oppressed be cared for and uplifted and that there be social justice for all. These ideas have not been part of Buddhism in Asia, but they are becoming an indelible aspect of Western Buddhism. So here too the Psalms have something to show us.

I would go so far as to say that for Western Buddhist practitioners, a sensitive and informed appreciation of the problematic themes included and so powerfully expressed in the Psalms is probably a necessity.

For many, however, the Psalms remain—as they did for me when I first encountered them in English at Gethsemani—hermetically sealed. This is because their language has become opaque after centuries of use and misuse. I am sure there are some (like the monks of Gethsemani and some Jewish practitioners I know) for whom the traditional language, illuminated by their inner experience, still sparkles, and the words take on added dimension with repeated encounter. But for most of the rest of us it is not so. For those who have not made a practice of the Psalms, the traditional language communicates little and can even be off-putting; for others, who read the Psalms but without much contemplation, the traditional language may still have meaning and emotion, but not much meaning that is spiritually fruitful.

So I wanted to use my own spiritual experience as my guide in reading and living with these most ancient of all poems, to try to make them fresh and lively for me and for readers like me.

The Psalms are poems. They stand at the origin point of all Western poetry, which is intimately connected with prayer.

I came to appreciate this about ten years ago, when I went to Jerusalem and visited the Kotel, the Wailing Wall. I had never been there before and was moved by the power of the place, with all its history, with all the prayer and lamentation that had gone into it from the lips of so many people over the generations. Although it had been many years since prayer had been a part of my spiritual practice, I found myself with my forehead pressed up against the cool stones, speaking heartfelt words and then writing words on a piece of paper and shoving the paper scrap into a crack in the wall, as people customarily do.

The feeling I had quite clearly was this: Making language is making prayer. Our utterances, whether silent or voiced, written or thought, distinct or vague, repeated or fleeting, are always essentially prayer, even though we seldom realize it. To speak, to intone, to form words with mouth and heart and spirit, is to reach out and reach in. What we're always reaching out and into, even when we don't know that we are, is the boundless unknowable, the unnameable. In the end prayer is not some specialized religious exercise; it is just what comes out of our mouths if we truly pay attention. Debased as it so often is, language at its core always springs forth from what is fundamental in the human heart.

If Buddhism makes sense, because it is strong on teachings that show us how to work with the mind and heart to relieve our suffering, it is at the same time perhaps weak on the question of relationships. Although our lives are located in our own hearts and minds, they are also located, perhaps most poignantly, in the space between us. Martin Buber's thought, his quintessentially Jewish outlook, emphasizes this with a fierce thoroughness. For Buber there is no God, no absolute, no present moment outside the profound relationship that takes place between the I and the you, between the self and the other. Within the hallowed reaches of that ineffable experience (which is not an experience, Buber insists) our true life takes place.

Relationship is the theme of the Psalms—specifically that most difficult of all relationships, the relationship with God.

What or who is God? The word *God*, with all its synonyms and substitutes as they appear in the Psalms, presents a serious problem for many. I find it meaningful and use it freely in my teaching, where it seems helpful (although it is absent in Zen language, and Zen is agnostic on the subject of God), but for many people the word *God* evokes parental and judgmental overtones and, even worse, false, meaningless, or even negative piety associated with what they have taken to be their less than perfect religious upbringings. In fact, the word *God* often seems to militate against exactly what it is supposed to connote, something immense and indescribable toward which one directs enormous feelings of awe, respect, gratitude, desire, anger, love, resentment, wonder, and so on.

For many of the religious seekers I encounter, the word *God* has been all but emptied of its spiritual power. Even where it is taken in a positive light it seems often reduced and tamed, representing some sort of assumed and circumscribed notion of holiness or morality. For me, what is challenging about "God" is exactly that it is so emotional, metaphysically emotional. The relationship to God that is charted out in the Psalms is a stormy one, codependent, passionate, confusing, loyal, petulant, sometimes even manipulative. I wanted to find a way to approach these poems so as to emphasize this relational aspect, while avoiding the major distancing pitfalls that words like *God*, *King*, *Lord*, and so on create. My solution was simple. I decided to avoid whenever I could all these words and instead use the one English word that best evokes the feeling of relationship, the word *you*.

Though I realize that the idea of seeing God as *you* isn't unique (it is a common trope in medieval Sufi poetry), it had a very personal, almost a private dimension for me. For some years I had been giving thought to the question of who the audience for my poetry actually was. I came to see that I was not writing for ordinary persons, not for colleagues, not for poetry lovers. The person to whom my poems actually seemed to be addressed was someone much more silent and much more profoundly receptive than any human being could possibly be. This person wasn't a person at all. It was nobody, nothing, and it wasn't anywhere or at any time. It was even beyond meaning. So poetry is important to me not because it gives me a chance to express myself, or to communicate, but because it is an encounter with that which is both so close to me I can't see it and so far away I can never reach it. Poetry evokes the unknowable.

Because of this, I have always found words themselves—the extraordinary fact of their being words—absolutely mysterious, especially words like *me* and *you* or *I*. Many of my poems hinge on the fundamental ineffability of such words and on the essentially incomprehensible nature of language itself, beyond its surface meanings. When we say "we" or "me" or "you" in a poem or elsewhere, do we really know what we mean? Shakespeare's sonnets, whose power comes from the fact that they are passionately addressed to a "you" who is forever unknown, have always impressed me, and I believe the whole sense of the lyric in Western poetry (beginning with the Psalms) has its source in this notion of a passionate writing addressed to a nonexistent or supraexistent listener. With human consciousness, with language, the perfect silence of being is necessarily broken as we call out with our words to one without a name or location, to all that immensity that surrounds us everywhere, inside us and outside us. The word *you* contains all that and includes all its sadness, intimacy, and power, for in the word *you* God becomes painfully close, utterly unreachable in his nearness.

There is certainly a theology implied in all this, and there are Buddhist roots to it. Although classical Buddhism emphasizes impermanence and nonself, clearly denies the existence of any abiding entity, and seems far from any feeling for a concept of God, with its overtones of omnipotence and eternity, the later Mahayana schools come very close to introducing the theistic. The Mind Only or Consciousness Only schools describe consciousness itself, in its profound transpersonal aspect, as Buddha Nature or Dharmakaya, neither existent nor nonexistent, neither inside nor outside, neither different from nor the same as the world, inconceivable. In the Chinese Shurangama Sutra, for instance, there are many passages exhorting practitioners to "turn the mind around" away from the world so that it can "revert" and realize its nature as eternally and inconceivably perfect. In the Lotus Sutra the Buddha reveals himself as a constant principle who only pretended to appear as a human being, teach the original doctrine, and die, for the sake of beings who were not able to understand the higher singular doctrine.

In the history of Buddhist philosophy there is an ongoing dialogue about the nature of such expressions. Since a cardinal principle of Buddhist thought is precisely that it be nontheistic, there has been continuous criticism of such doctrines, contending that they are subversive attempts to introduce the concept of God into the Buddhist system of thought. The Mind Only adherents defend themselves by replying that their conception of consciousness doesn't violate the principle of emptiness, which states that all things are mere designations, without substance, like a mirage, so consciousness cannot be said to be a God. I am surely not doing justice to this complex debate, but the point I am trying to make is that such Buddhist speculations (the Shurangama Sutra even includes, un-Buddhistically, a detailed section on the creation of the mind and the physical world out of the original primordial nameless consciousness) are not far removed from many Jewish and Christian discussions of the idea of God.

The Psalms are historical documents of a particular people whose sacred narrative stands behind every line. My dilemma in making versions that I considered useful to me and to others like me was how to preserve the emotion of that peoplehood and history yet at the same time widen it. Although the Jewish and Christian commentarial literature on the Psalms opens and expands them into a more universal application, translated versions I have read do not attempt to fold those interpretations into the poems themselves. This is what I wanted to attempt. So, how to handle these historical and particular words?

I began with the obvious fact that words like *Israel, Zion, Jerusalem,* and so on originally carried meanings beyond their limited later senses. In other words, if Israel became a nation, what was the original impulse or spiritual dynamic that made it that? If Jerusalem is a holy city existing in a particular location, what is the content of that holiness? More often than not what I was looking for could be found in looking closely at the etymologies of the words themselves. So *Israel* means "one who struggles," who for me is the ideal of a certain type of spiritual seeker, one whose faithfulness is always full of doubt, one forever pressing on with the practice, for new and fresh insight, for deeper experience. So I rendered the word *Israel* usually as "the ones who question and struggle." *Jerusalem* means "the place of wholeness," the place where the soul can feel free and complete. Egypt, by contrast, is "the narrow place."

With these ideas to start with, I looked at each psalm for the way a particular term functioned within it and at a number of psalms to see how that term was developed throughout the collection. As I worked on this, I began to have a feeling for the spiritual and literary movement and shape of the terms, and they took on a depth of meaning for me that they had not had before. In my versions I sometimes retain the original words, sometimes replace them with what I think are their spiritual analogues, and sometimes use both, depending on the context and on the sound and sense in English.

. . .

Respiritualizing some of the political and geographical references in the Psalms brought up for me the wider question of what was behind these references. From a Buddhist perspective, Judeo-Christian spirituality is challenging indeed. As I have said, Buddhism teaches suffering and the end of suffering. This seems a far cry from the personal and political anguish and group catharsis that one sees throughout the Psalms. It made me wonder, What does all this amount to? If I assume the spiritual path to be more or less general throughout the traditions, what could the drama of the Psalms be pointing toward?

The idea of sovereignty seems to me to be one of the key themes of the Psalms. God is the ultimate fountain-head of sovereignty. Through God sovereignty is con-ferred on the kings, and through them in turn to the people. With sovereignty there is honor, reality, a se-cure place to be, the possibility of wholeness and salva-tion, a way to live. With sovereignty exile in the world ends, and one comes home.

The most powerful Psalms seem to yearn for the sovereignty that only God can confer, to praise it where it is present, to lament it where it is gone, and to evoke constantly God's presence and praise God's name—all because of the potency of sovereignty. I have pondered this, investigated it for what I could begin to see of its spiritual content, and have finally formed a notion of sovereignty as spiritual authenticity: some deeply felt but almost indefinable quality of meaningfulness that is the highest potential of human experience. It is as if a human being exists but doesn't live, is physically present but spiritually dead, if this quality of sovereignty is absent.

This thinking personalized for me all those passages in the Psalms that deal with praise and gratefulness to God and with kingship and political tragedy, and it gave me a way to understand the difficult passages, the so-called cursing psalms. While I did not want to make things too pretty, turning outward enemies into internal demons and making curses into gentle reminders toward self-improvement, I did think in the end that the Psalms' historical narrative and poetic drama of sovereignty was also personal and spiritual.

As I considered the issue of sovereignty, I began to see a connection in the Psalms between it and the Buddhist notion of mindfulness. The Mindfulness Sutra calls mindfulness the only way to liberation. As you read that text, with all its careful instructions for training, it is clear that what is pointed to differs from the conventional notion of mindfulness, which amounts more or less to self-consciousness: I know that I am feeling this or sensing that; I know that I am myself and not another. This is how we generally understand mindfulness. But Buddhist mindfulness is, by contrast, a resting in a level of consciousness that is antecedent to the experience of ego or to any notion of separation from the world. It is an appreciation of all that is arising within the field of consciousness, without defining an inside or an outside.

I began to think that the sovereignty of God referred to in the Psalms was a species of consciousness, beyond the human yet not separate from it, a kind of settled and steady contemplation of or union with the deity constantly evoked and longed for in the poems. If that were so, I had a way of understanding concepts like wickedness and punishment. Wickedness became heedlessness, unmindfulness, egotism, off-centeredness, crookedness. To fall into such a state is to suffer alienation, to be off course and terrified. Sin becomes a question of being off the mark, of being a distance away from the unity that one finds within mindfulness, and punishment for sin is natural and necessary if there is to be a course correction. I came to think that the enemies mentioned in the Psalms were external but also internal. Praying for their defeat could be seen to be akin to praying, as in Tibetan Buddhism, to fierce guardian deities to destroy the powerful inner passions that keep one in bondage. Certainly I do not want to claim the Psalms as Buddhist texts. But such reflections helped me understand their passion in a new light.

Despite all this, I do not think that the difficulty of the Psalms can in the end be entirely avoided or explained away. Earlier I mentioned that many of the brothers at Gethsemani offered good explanations of why the difficulty was necessary and in the end positive. There are, however, many other committed Christians and Jews who feel there can be no good justification for the violence and passion of the Psalms, believing that for liturgical practice and theological discussion the Psalms ought to be edited, spiritually objectionable passages dropped, and whole psalms eliminated altogether. There has been an ongoing debate about this for some years within the Catholic monastic community, and as a result, some monasteries have made their own versions of the psaltery.

That the Psalms' difficulty, their violent and uncompromising spirit, can have tragic consequences came home to me recently. I was in Belfast, Northern Ireland, at a peace conference, listening to a panel of speakers who were victims of the "troubles," as they are called. One was a woman who had been confined to a wheelchair for most of her adult life as a result of a drive-by political shooting. There was a man who had been blinded as a boy by a British bullet. Another man, who had taken part in assassinations, described how his spirit had been crushed by what he had done. Each person spoke of how his or her suffering had been a difficult but ultimately important road toward purification, forcing him or her to find alternatives to bitterness and despair. Each of them seemed somehow to be a happy person, living a productive life, and all of them were engaged in peace or social work of one kind or another.

There was one exception. This was a Protestant minister whose father, a policeman, had been gunned down in his own home, while his family, including the minister, then a teenage boy, stood by helplessly. Unlike the other speakers, the minister did not express any sense of forgiveness or serenity about what had happened to him. Instead he seemed to affirm strong feelings of hatred and vengeance as being natural and even positive. He said that after many years of anguish he had recently come to some satisfaction because he had found evidence indicating that his father's killers had themselves been gunned down by other assassins.

He said that it made him finally happy to know that justice had finally been done, as God wished. His speech was the briefest and seemed to be the least warmly engaged with the audience. In concluding it, he quoted from memory Psalm 10, which includes a line about how God will break the arms of the wicked. This strong expression of righteous vengeance had sustained and inspired the minister all these many years.

I want finally to mention one further influence that stands behind the efforts I have been making with the Psalms. This is my reading of the Jewish German-language poet Paul Celan, a deeply spiritual and inward writer, a Holocaust survivor, whose works are an attempt to meet the tremendous challenge to the human spirit that that event (to which Celan refers as only "what happened") occasioned. Celan uses biblical material (including the Psalms) with all the traditional feeling it evokes, yet at the same time manages to make it personal, as if the ancient lines and their echoes were coming from his own mouth for the first time, expressing the depth of all he had seen and experienced himself. Writing in German, the language of the murderer and oppressor, he could not help recognizing with each word how easily language betrays us even as it provides us with the emotional and religious connection to that which we most need in our extremity. In time Celan's poems became more and more terse, more and more dense, until by the end of his short life (he committed suicide in Paris in 1970, in his forty-ninth year) they were all but incomprehensible, approaching closely the boundary of what can be said.

Celan's project as a writer is the desperate attempt to find meaning in a terrible situation, one in which a return to an innocent or traditional faith seems impossible. This is why it is so important for our time, in which it is the challenge of religious traditions to do something more than simply reassert and reinterpret their faiths, hoping for loyal adherents to what they perceive to be the true doctrine. Looking back at the last century, with its devastating wars and holocausts and the shock of ecological vulnerability, I have the sense that religious traditions must now take on a wider mission, and it is in recognition of this mission, I believe, that interreligious dialogue becomes not only something polite and interesting but essential. I have come to think, after working for many years intimately with many people along the course of their heartfelt spiritual journeys, that traditions now need to listen to the human heart before them as much as and more than they listen to their various doctrines and beliefs. In recognition of this I offer these tentative versions of the Psalms.

The Psalms

HappY is the one who walks otherwise
Than in the manner of the heedless
Who stands otherwise
Than in the way of the twisted
Who does not sit in the seat of the scornful
But finds delight in the loveliness of things
And lives by that pattern all day and all night—

For this one is like a tree planted near a stream
That gives forth strong fruit in season
And whose leaf doesn't wither
And whose branches spread wide—

Not so the heedless

They are like chaff scattered by the wind
Endlessly driven, they cannot occupy their place
And so can never be seen or embraced
And they can never be joined

What you see is always lovely and remembered
But the way of heedlessness is oblivion

Psalm

1

WHAT MAKES NATIONS ERUPT and people's minds go
    wild?

Psalm 2

The heedless take counsel of the heedless
And in their senselessness think to flee from you
And from the authority only you confer, saying
"Let us break apart the ties
And throw away the cords"

You laugh at them, hold them up in derision
You speak your anger for them, terrifying them in your
    confoundedness:

I have ordained what is as it utterly is
On Zion, this mountain where you stand
Announcing the order of things in clear words:
That you are my children, repeatedly created as I am now
And that what you with rounded words pronounce
I will grant
The nations are for you only, your immediate birthright
You possess and are possessed by all and everywhere
And so you break oppression like a rod of iron is broken
And you crush heedlessness as a potter's vessel is crushed
    underfoot

And you who think that flight from me is possible
That it is protection, advancement, and power—
Take warning in these words:

Recognize the sovereignty of what is
Recognize it with awesome respect
Rejoice in it, but with care
Pay homage to it, but without greed
Lest the unnameable consume you in the leaping flames
Of loneliness, dispossession, and hatred

      Happy are they who find their home
      In the kingdom of what is

How MANY ARE my tormentors
How many rise up against me
How many say of me, "There is no hope for him"

But you
Are a shield around me
A shield of brilliant light
So I hold my head high

With my voice I call out to you
And your silent comfort rolls out from the holy mountain
And when I lie down to sleep
You contain me and I rise up again

I am not afraid of the threatening thousands

Rise up and embrace me!
Shatter the jaws, break the teeth of my torment
That no twisted words can be formed in its mouth

Salvation flows from you
And blessings rain down on your people

Because I call
You answer
For you are fitting
Because I am small
You enlarge me
For you are gracious
You hear my song

How long will the others
Darken my light
How long will they
Live in uselessness
Lies and seduction
Knowing you set aside
The good for your own
And answer me when I call

People, tremble
And be upright
Commune with your hearts
In the deep of night
Awake on your beds

Be still:
Offer that
For it is fitting
Trust it
For it is the rightness
Of all that is

People say
Who will bring us
What we need?
Who will beam

Psalm
4

Heaven's light
On us?

But already
My heart has more joy
Than full granaries
And wineries
Could provide

And I will lie down
To sleep
With a deep peace
For in you
I find my completion

LISTEN
Incline your ear toward me
Listen to my piercing cry as I pray
At daybreak hear my voice
When I order my words toward you
              And wait

For you do not take pleasure in the crooked
The heedless can never reach your courts
The arrogant fall away when you look at them
The wicked are distasteful to you
Liars you cut off
The violent ones, the deceivers, you cast away

But as for me—
Bathed in your encircling kindness I enter your house
Bow myself down before your presence
In awe and wonder

Lead me into rightness against the force of my envy
Straighten me
For their mouths know not a single sincere word
Inside they are full of deception
Their throats are graves
Their tongues slides
Cast them out of me
Let them fall by their own weight all the way down
For they are your counterforce

Then all who put their trust in you will rejoice
Will shout out their joy in your protection
Will exalt in you all who love your unsayableness
For you bless the faithful
Circling them round like a shield

DON'T CRUSH ME with your anger

Don't singe me with your flame
But be gracious, for I am diminishing
And heal me, for I am terrified even to the bones of my
    body
And my heart is seared, and my soul shrinks

        And you: how long
        How long O Lord, how long?

Turn now
O turn and revolve my soul

This is the work of your natural kindness
For in faithless death there's no one to remember you
And in mute narrowness no one to sing your
    thanksgiving songs

I am exhausted from my sighing
Every night my bed's a lake of sorrow
A drowning flood of tears and sweat
My eyes are blind with grieving
They become weak with the force against me

        You now leave me, narrowness and
            blindness!
        For the voice of my weeping has been heard!

My lamentation has turned into courage
Now the narrowness that pressed against me is startled
Suddenly it is turned—shamed and disarmed—

Your unsayable name: it covers all the earth
And your presence extends ever outward
From the furthest conceivable point

Out of the mouths of babes
Who speak only wordless wondering words
You fashion your incomprehensible power
That gathers into silence all opposition
All that pressure to deaden and destroy

When I behold the night sky, the work of your fingers
The bright moon and the many-layered stars which you
    have established
I think:

A woman is so frail and you remember her
A man so small and you think of him

And yet
In you woman and man become as angels
Crowned with a luminous presence
And you have given them care for the works of your hands
Placed the solid growing earth under their feet

Flocks of birds and herds of deer
Oxen and sheep and goats and cows
Soaring birds and darting fishes
All that swims the paths of the sea

O you whom I am ever addressing
Your unsayable name covers heaven and earth

WHY DO YOU STAND ALOOF
Hiding yourself in troubled times?

The heedless in their arrogance pursue the lowly
And catch them with their subtle devices
The heedless flaunt their appetites
In their grasping they bless themselves
And despise you
His arrogance is this:
That he thinks you are not watching
Nowhere in all his schemes does he account for you
He is always prosperous—
Whatever affliction you are reserving for him
Is far away for now
So he snorts at his adversaries
Saying to himself, I will not be moved
I will live forever without any trouble
His mouth is full of false promises deceit and fraud
Under his tongue are mischief and misdeeds
He hides in the shadows and alleyways of the villages
Murders the innocent in these out-of-the-way places
His eyes always watching out for the lowly
He lies in wait in the secret places
Like a lion in his den
Lies in wait to snatch up the lowly
And he snatches them up when they're drawn into his
    trap
He crouches, he bends down low to deceive them
And they are deceived by his deceptions
He thinks in his heart that you have forgotten him
That you have hidden away your face
That you aren't watching, will not see

Stir yourself!
Lift your hand!

Do not forget the sufferers!
Why should the heedless go on being heedless?
Why should they continue to think in their hearts
That you are not watching?

You *are* watching!
You see all trouble and misaction
You give it its due with your own hand
The sufferer relies on you
The unprotected counts on your help
Break the arm of the heedless one
Search out his callousness thoroughly
Till there isn't any left

You are sovereign endlessly
All lesser powers pass away
You hear the longing of the sufferers
And make them strong
By your listening
Knowing the unprotected and oppressed as they
    actually are
And thus no mortal of the earth can be arrogant

I HAVE TRUSTED YOU—
How can you say to my soul
"Take flight like a mountain bird?"

Can't you see
Crookedness bending its bow
Setting its arrow on the string
To shoot in the dark
At the upright heart?

When the foundation crumbles
What is right?

You are in your holy temple
Reclining on your heavenly throne
Yet your eye still sees us
Your gaze still proves us

I know you prove the upright
But crookedness and violence—
These your soul casts off
You hurl burning coals at them
Fire and brimstone you rain down
And from their cup they drink
The flaming ripping wind

For you are where rightness is
Rightness is your loving-kindness
Your face glows with it

I CALL OUT TO YOU
For the real is gutted
The truth has fallen away
From the human family
And self-deceit and small advantage corrupt speech

Between neighbor and neighbor subtle lies weave
      entangling threads
They speak with a heart and a heart beside that heart
Even their own hearts they unknowingly deny

Cut off all nattering lips
The self-doubtful tongue that speaks a twisted
      language
Saying, "With our words we'll be mighty
We'll speak as we wish,
Our words are ours to fashion"

And you reply,
"Because of the oppression of the poor
Because of the sighs of the needy
I will rise up
I will grant them safety
For whom the others have laid a snare
By the self-deceit of their words"

Your words
Are straight, clear, shining
As silver refined in earth's crucible
Seven times purified—
You will deliver them, guard them
From the generation of the lie
Always—

For when the lie is raised up
The wicked walk proudly on every side
As if the world were made for them

How LONG WILL YOU PERSIST in forgetting me?

Psalm

How long will you hide your face?

13

How long do I have to drive my soul on
With useless heartache and grief?
How long will my detractors laugh at my manufactured
   troubles?

Look down, answer me—
Brighten my eyes so they won't sink into deadness
So that my detractors won't say
"Look, we have deceived him"
So that they won't rejoice as I slip out of sight

I trust your kindness—
Gladden my heart with your responding
And I will sing your songs
In this sudden opening to you

THE USELESS FOOL SAYS in his heart
"God is nothing"
People are corrupt, do only harm
Not one does good unselfishly, not one

You gaze down from the highest
Upon humankind in the middle
To see if there is one person with eyes
One with understanding
One capable of seeing your seeing

But they are all gone bad
All turned sour and blind
There is none who knows good
Not one

Is there not even a speck of understanding
In all the world of blind heedlessness
Among those who eat up others as if they were bread
And do not even know their own hearts
Or a single true word?

But they become terrified even within their terror
When they see you burning in the circle of goodness
Shining out of the eyes of the lowly and the poor
Showing your holiness in their defeat
Your invincible power at the center of their weakness .

O that someone might come out of Zion
To bring freedom to the strugglers!

When you capture the people again
The sojourners will be glad
And the strugglers will rejoice with strong singing

Who can rest in your tent?
Who can stand on your mountain?

The one who walks upright
Does what is good
Utters true words of the heart
And does not deceive with the tongue
Who does no harm to a neighbor
And never reproaches others
Who sees crookedness for what it is
And honors the truth that flows from you
Whose word is firm even in difficulty
Who gives asking nothing in return
And does not seek advantage
At the expense of the innocent

The one who lives this way
Will never be shaken

Protect me from fear
For I place my trust only in you
My soul has said, "You are my guardian
Sole foundation of my happiness
And I will find my delight
In all that is yours on earth"

As for all that shuts you out—
Great will be their sorrow
I will not pour out their offerings
Nor call their names even in my dreams

You, you, only you

Are my share and my cup
You have drawn my lot
And it has fallen out agreeably

Lovely indeed is my estate
My heritage is pleasant to me
I bless you who brought me to this day
And even at night in the trying times
My trembling body is tethered to you

Your presence is always before me
In all the deeds of my hand
I will not be shaken from it
So my heart rejoices
My spirit is glad
And my body rests secure

For you will not abandon my soul to the darkness
You will not suffer me to be overwhelmed in terror
You will teach me the path toward life

Your presence is my sweetest joy
Your right hand my chief delight

Always

Hear the justice of my case
Heed my plea
Give ear to my prayer
Uttered with lips that do not pronounce deceit
Let my sentence come forth from your presence
For yours are truth-seeing eyes

You have proven my heart
Thought of me in the long night
Refined and tempered me till nothing impure remained
And my words and intentions were straight and
     altogether true

Guided by your words
I saw in the world
All the dissolute paths
My steps trod only your byways
And my foot did not slip

So I call on you now
Knowing you will answer—
Incline your ear toward me, hear my words
Show the wonder of your kindness
You who save those who trust you
From those who rise up against them
With your right hand

Guard me like the apple of your eye
Hide me in the shadow of your wings
From my assailants who want to sap my strength
And are everywhere about me

They are muffled by their successes
They mouth arrogance and self-pride

Now they are standing in my footsteps
Now they look out at the land through my eyes
Like lions eager for meat
Lurking in the hidden places

Arise, go forth to meet him
Prevent him, cast him out
Snatch me from the grip of the crooked
Who is your sword
From these debasers—who are your hand—

From the world
Whose portion is in this fleeting life
And whose belly you fill with your hidden treasures
So that they have many children
And they pass on their wealth to them

As for me—
        I will encounter you in my faithfulness
        I will be satisfied
        Filled with a quiet vision of you

I love you, O God, my strength
You are my cliff, my fortress, my champion
Rock on whom I build my house
My shield, trumpet of my salvation
My towering spire
I shout out praise to you
And am saved
The ropes of death bound me
Floods of devastation terrified me
Ropes of darkness cut into me
Snares of death entrapped me
In my distress I called out to you
To you I cried desperately
And from your temple
You heard my voice
My bitter complaint reached your ear
And the earth rocked and trembled
The foundations of the mountains shook
Split open by your anger
Smoke billows plumed out
Devouring fire flamed up
Burning coals shot forth from you
And the sky bent and you arrived
Thick darkness under your feet
Riding a cloud, soaring
Darting along on the wind's wings
You hid yourself in darkness
Round about you swirled black thunderheads
Thick black beasts of the sky
From the blinding brilliance before you
These thick clouds were driven on
With icy hailstones and blazing coals
And the sky thundered deafeningly
And your voice boomed with hail and coals

Psalm 18

And the sky shot blazing arrows and scattered them
Shot flashing lightnings and drove them off
And the ocean beds were exposed like entrails
The foundations of the world laid open like wounds
Through your roaring
At the blast of the breath of your nostrils
You reached down and snatched me
Drew me out of the foaming waters
Delivered me from my enemy
The hatred that was too strong for me
That overcame me on the day of my calamity
But you were my support
And brought me forth into a large space
Saved me because I was your delight
You rewarded my rightness
Reached out to my open hands
For I have always heeded you
Have never slipped from your path
Your ways have always been before me
Nothing have I ignored or denied
I have been upright
Guarding myself against crookedness and deception
Therefore you requited me according to my rightness
According to the openness of my hands before your eyes
To the kind you are kindness
To the upright uprightness
To the pure purity
And for the perverse you provide difficulty
For you will surely save the sufferers
But the high and mighty you bring down
You will cause my light to shine
You will illuminate my darkness
With you I will break through enemy lines
With you I will scale prison walls

Your way is perfect, your word true
You shield all who trust you
Who else can protect them?
You who made me iron
You who removed all my obstructions
You who gave me deer's legs
You who made me stand in the high places
Who trained my hands for the struggle
Who made my arms strong to bend a bronze bow
And gave me your unbreachable shield
And held me up with your right hand
Whose attention has made me great
Who made my steps swift and sure
So that I never slip
And when I pursue my enemies I overtake them
And I do not run back until I make an end of them
I uproot them entirely so they can never rise up
They fall under my onrushing feet
You who have given me the power to struggle
Who hurl my enemies under my feet
Who cause them to turn and run from me
All that hatred—entirely gone—
They cry out but no one helps them
To you but you don't answer them
And they are beaten fine as windswept dust
Like dirt they are swept off the streets
You who have removed me from desire's contentions
Who have made me sovereign among nations
That all shall honor me
As soon as their ears hear my words they heed
The children of the stranger pledge loyalty to me
Their opposition fades away
They come tumbling out of their hiding places
Into the light of day

Like bees from a hive in the sunlight
Only you live, blessed, my rock
Exalted, my protection
Only you who lifted me up
And placed all my hatred under me
You who saved me from hatred
And lifted me high above it
Who delivered me safe from violence
Therefore I will give all thanks to you
And I will sing songs to your unsayableness
To you who gave me sovereignty
Who anointed me with loving-kindness
David and his seed
Always

THE HEAVENS EXPRESS your fire
The night sky is the work of your hands
Day after day is your spoken language
Night after night your perfect knowing
There is no speech, there are no words
Their voice falls silent
Yet the music plays everywhere
To the end of the earth its clear notes float out
To the end of the worlds the words pronounced
Become a tabernacle for the sun
That comes out like a bridegroom from his chamber
A robust runner to run his day's course
To the end of the heavens he races
And back again he returns
And there is nothing hidden from his heat

Your pattern is perfection
It quiets the soul that knows it
And its eloquent expression
Makes everything clear
So that even the simple are wise

Your ways are upright
Making the heart glad
Your distances are clear
Washing out the eyes
Your awesomeness is pure
And endures constantly
What you require is just
For it is nothing but the truth
And it is more durable than the finest gold
Sweeter than the drippings of the honeycomb
Who serves you is inspired
And in following you finds reward

Psalm 19

Who is free from all error?
You take hold of it and turn it right
And where there is confusion
Let me not become entangled
And I will be blameless
Clear of any misdirection

May these words of my mouth
And these meditations of my heart
Be acceptable to you
My rock, my release

In trouble
Answer us—
Let your unsayableness
(Jacob's mystery)
Protect us
Sending us help from the holy places
Support from Zion

Accept and remember our offerings
Accept and honor our burnt sacrifice
Grant what our hearts yearn for
Fulfill our resolve

We rejoice in your meeting us
And we go out to meet you
With your nameless name scrawled on our banners—
Fulfill our petitions

I know now
That the dedicated ones
Will feel your saving grace
That you will answer them from the heavens
Will lift up your right arm

Some trust in chariots, some in horses
But we trust your namelessness
They lie prostrate, fallen
But we rise up, standing erect

O be our savingness
Be our kingliness, our dignity
Now as we call out to your calling

SOVEREIGNTY SHINES THROUGH your power
The king exults in your victories
You grant the heart's most royal desire
Answer the lips' most regal request
You meet them unasked with anointments of happiness
And place on their heads a golden crown

Life cries out for endlessness
And you grant it
Greatly honored it is in your presence
Wreathed in splendor and bountiful light
You offer it as a continual blessing
Grace it with your presence, your joy

The king puts all his trust in you
And rooted in your kindness
He shall not be moved

Your hand reaches out to the adversaries
Your right hand touches them
Setting them ablaze like a furnace
You anger igniting them with passionate flames
Cauterizing their fruit so it won't ripen
Scouring their seed so it can't sprout

For they confounded you
Set in motion a counterpurpose
Which they could not carry out

You turn them around so they face you
Draw them back like a taut bow
Your piercing arrows aimed within their eyes

The strength of your saving sovereignty lifts you up!
We sing in praise of your power

My God, my God, why have you forsaken me?
Why so far from my delivery
So empty in the anguish of my words?
I call to you in the daytime but you don't answer
And all night long I plead restlessly, uselessly

I know your holiness, find it in the memorized praises
Uttered by those who've struggled with you
Through all the generations
These, my forebears, trusted you
And through their trusting you touched them
Held and delivered them
They cried out to you and you met them face to face
Their confidence was strong and they were not
    confounded

But I am not as they
Utterly alone, I am cast out of the circle
A worm, a living reproach, scorned and despised, even
    less than despised
Unheard, unseen, unacknowledged, denied
And all who encounter me revile me with cynic
    laughter
Shaking their heads, parting their nattering lips,
    mocking
"Let him throw himself at God for his deliverance,"
    they say
"Since that is who he trusts let the Lord save him."

And they are right:
How not trust you, and what else to trust?

You I entered on leaving the womb
You I drank at my mother's breast

I was cast upon you at birth
And even before birth I swam in you, my heart's darkness

Be not far from me now
When suffering is very near
And there is no help
And I am beset all round by threatening powers
The bulls of Bashan gaping their dismal braying mouths
Their ravenous roaring lion mouths

I am poured out like water
My bones' joints are snapped like twigs
My heart melts like wax
Flooding my bowels with searing viscid emotion
My strength is dried up like a potsherd
My tongue cleaves woolly to the roof of my mouth
And I feel my body dissolving into death's dusts

For I am hounded by my isolation
Am cast off and encircled by the assembly of the violent
Who like vicious dogs snap at my hands and feet
I count the bones of my naked body
As the mongrels shift and stare and circle
They divide my clothes among themselves, casting lots
     for them

So now in this very place I call on you
There is no one left

Do not be far from me
Be the center
Of the center
Of the circle
Be the strength of that center

The power of the absence that is the center
Deliver my life from the killing sharpnesses
Deliver my soul from the feverish dogs
Save me from the lion mouths
Answer me with the voice of the ram's horn

And I will seek and form and repeat your name among
    my kinsmen
In the midst of everyone I will compose praises with
    my lips
And those who enter your awesomeness through my
    words will also praise
All the seed of Jacob will glorify you
And live in awe of you
All those who question and struggle
Will dawn with your light
For they will know
You have not scorned the poor and despised
Nor recoiled disgusted from their faces
From them your spark has never been hidden
And when they cried out in their misery
You heard and answered and ennobled them
And it is the astonishment of this that I will praise in
    the Great Assembly
Making deep vows in the presence of those who know
    your heart
Know that in you the meek eat and are satisfied
And all who seek and struggle find the tongue to praise
Saying to you:

May your heart live forever
May all the ends of the earth remember and return to you
And all the families of all the nations bow before you
For all that is is your domain

Your flame kindles all that lives and breathes
And you are the motive force of all activity
The yearning of the grasses, the lovers' ardor
And they that rise up, live, and eat the fat of the earth
    will bow before you
Before you will bow all those who lie down, find peace,
    and enter the dust
For none can keep alive by his own power—you alone
    light the soul
Distant ages to come shall serve you, shall be related to
    you in future times
Those people not yet born
Will sing of your uprightness, your evenness, your
    brightness
To a people not yet born that is still yet to come
That this is how you are

YOU ARE MY SHEPHERD, I am content
You lead me to rest in the sweet grasses
To lie down by the quiet waters
And I am refreshed

You lead me down the right path
The path that unwinds in the pattern of your name

And even if I walk through the valley of the shadow of
    death
I will not fear
For you are with me
Comforting me with your rod and your staff
Showing me each step

You prepare a table for me
In the midst of my adversity
And moisten my head with oil

Surely my cup is overflowing
And goodness and kindness will follow me
All the days of my life
And in the long days beyond
I will always live within your house

ALL THE EARTH AND ALL that fills it belongs to you
And the earth and all that lives is yours
For you have arrayed it upon the dark waters
Upon the rivers you have set it firm

Who shall ascend your mountain?
Who shall stand in the place where you stand?

The one with open hands
The one with a quiet heart
The one whose soul is not lifted up with lies
Nor deceit, seduction, or heedlessness

That one will be moved along with your blessing
Will be fortified with your rightness
And will be kept whole

This is the circle of those who love you
Who search out your presence
Jacob's family: those who journey

Raise your heads, gates!
Be raised wide, everlasting doors
And let the fire enter!
What is this fire?
It is you, powerful and final
Decisive in all things

Raise up your heads, gates!
Raise open wide, everlasting doors
And let the fire in!
What is this fire?
All in all, this is the fire
All in all, this is what burns ever bright

Now as I sing
I lift up my soul to you
I open my heart's trust
Do not let me be ashamed
Do not let it close

I know that no one who trusts
Will ever be ashamed
Let them be ashamed
Who uselessly deceive
Because they are deceived

Show me your ways
Teach me your paths
Lead me in your truthfulness
Teach me
For in you I am whole
And on you do I wait
All the day every day

Remember your tender mercies
Remember your encompassing kindness
Which is everlasting

But forget my youthful mistakes
Forget all the harm that I have done
According to your kindness
Hold me in your memory
For the sake of all that is good in me

For you are goodness and uprightness
You point out the way of wholeness
Guide the still soul on paths of justice
You teach her your pattern

All your paths are kindness and truth
For those who love you and hold you in mind

For the sake of your unsayableness
Forgive my confusion although it is great

Who feels awe at what is?
To those will you point out
The paths that they should choose
And their souls will abide in a happiness
Larger than their lives
Your secrets are for those awash in that awe
Your life will become known to them

My eyes always look on you
You draw my foot out of the snare
Turn toward me and be gracious
For I am alone and afflicted
My heart's burdens are heavy

O bring me out of these afflictions!
Look at my misery and my trouble
Lift the weight of my conduct from me
Defeat my many demons
Pacify the violence within me
Guard me and save me
Don't let me be ashamed

I put all my trust in you
Let integrity and uprightness guard me
Because I look only to you
Redeem me and those who struggle on the journey
From our pitiful distress

YOU ARE MY LIGHT and my help
        Whom should I fear?
You are the fortress of my life
        Whom should I dread?
When the narrow ones gather their strength to
   devour me
        It is they who stumble and fall
Even if a royal army were camped outside my gate
        My heart would not fear
And when they struck out with terrible weapons
   against me
        Even then I'd trust

One thing I ask for, one thing I hope—
        To live in your house
        All the days of my life
        To behold your loveliness
        Every morning in the light of your temple
           dawn

Till on a doomful day
You secure me in your precincts
Conceal me within the folds of your covering tent
Place me high and safe upon a rock
My head lifted above the engulfing waves

With the joy of my heart
I will sacrifice
Within that billowing shelter
Singing and playing my abandonment to you

Hear my voice when I raise it up
Be gracious—answer me—

**Psalm
27**

Speaking with your voice my heart sang,
Seek my presence

I will

Do not hide your glowing face from me
Do not reject me in anger because of my shortcomings
You have always been for me
Don't cast me off now, don't walk away
My helper, my friend

My mother and father forsake me
But you take me up
Show me the way!
Guide my steps on the clear path
Against the ever-present cliffs and thickets
Protect me from the noise of desire and hatefulness
From false words and shouted accusations

If I did not have faith in your rightness
That it would bloom in this living land—
It is unthinkable

I wait only for you
With strength and good courage—

I wait only for you

I CALL OUT TO YOU, my rock
Don't turn unheeding from me
For if you silent move away
I will be like one fallen down
Into a dark cold pit

Hear my voice reaching outward
When it cries for you
When I lift up my hands
Toward your holiness
Don't mistake me
Don't sweep me away with the crooked
With the heedless ones
Who speak pleasingly with their neighbors
But have hidden mischief in their hearts

Give them the just results of their actions
Reward them according to the work of their hands
Bestow on them what they deserve
Because they don't see your ways
Don't care about the work of your hands
Let them fall down
Let them not build up

Gratitude to you
Who are the hearing of my outreaching words
My strength and shield
In whom my heart trusts
And I am helped
And my heart enraptures
And I sing thanksgiving songs to you
Who are the strength of all who love you

The fortress of those dedicated to you
Help us, bless our ongoingness
Feed our hearts
Open us up in the timeless days

O HIGH AND MIGHTY ONES
Glory and strength are not yours
They belong to another
To the unsayable name
Offer what you have
To that holiness
Ascribe all your works

Your voice is the voice of the waters
When they thunder as foaming towers
Those plunging waters, those swelling words
Your voice booms out its power
It sings with majesty
Breaking the cedars to splinters
And the cedars of Lebanon shiver to hear it
They skip like calves
Lebanon and Syria like frightened rams
Your voice blasts columns of wildfire
That shake the wilderness
The wilderness of Kadesh trembling with flames
And the deer run off in terror
And the forests are scorched bare
And in your house
People speak of nothing but your terrible force

You sat unmoving in the flood time
Your sitting is sovereign and constant
And you reflect this strength in our inmost hearts
So that we may be blessed with peace

I will lift you up
As you have lifted me
Up from my oppressors
That they might not rejoice at my lowliness

In my crying out to you
I was healed

You raised up my soul from the depths
Repaired my wings that I should not go down
To the pit of despair

All who live in gratefulness
Sing thanks to remember your holiness
For though your anger flashes out suddenly
Your hands are gentle, they hold all of life

In the evening weeping comes and it remains for a night
But with the morning light comes joyful song

When all was well with me I said
"I shall never be shaken"
For your favor made me mountain-firm

But then you hid from me
And I was terrified

Now I call out to you with these words
Meeting you in my spoken humility

What profit is there in my blood
When I go down to the grave?
Will the dust speak your praises?
Will it strain like me to utter your truth?

Hear my words, respond, help me—

      You have changed my grieving into dancing!
      Thrown off my mourning clothes and
          dressed me in joy
      So that my whole being might sing to you
          without ceasing
      Pouring out my gratitude without end

In you I put my trust
Let me never be ashamed—
Release me in your rightness
Bend your ear to me
Deliver me quickly
Be my rock of protection
Like a mountain my stronghold of safety
You are my rock and my stronghold
For the sake of your unsayableness
Lead me, guide me
Draw me out of the net
Set within the secret darkness
For you are my protection
I put my soul in your hands
And you hold it fast in your truth
From those that depend on deceit
I hasten away
Trusting indeed in you
I will gladly rejoice in your kindness
Because you have seen my misery
And have not turned your face away
You have known the distress of my soul
And have not abandoned me to adversity
Have given me an ample space on which to stand
Be gracious for I am in distress
My eye is consumed with restless clinging
My body twists and my soul writhes
For my life is exhausted with dissatisfaction
My years are like broken sighs
My strength fails because of my inner trials
Even my bones grow thin
To all my assailants I am an insult
To my neighbors an embarrassment
To my friends a horror

When they see me on the street they run away
I am as forgotten as the dead
As unremembered as a broken pot
I heard the whispering of many
Terror assailed me on every side
As they spoke of a plot against me
But my trust in you was strong
I said, "You are my ruler
In your hand is my destiny"
Deliver me from their hands
Snatch me away from those who wish me harm
Shine the light of your eye on me
And save me through your kindness
Do not let me be put to shame
Unworthy and out of your sight
For I have called out to you with these words
Let the adversary be put to shame
Let him be eclipsed in silence
Passing into dark unspeakable worlds
Let the lying lips be stilled
That speak harsh words against the faithful
With pride and contempt
O how great is your goodness
Which you have treasured up for the faithful
Which you use on behalf of those who trust you
In the face of humankind
You will conceal them within your hidden presence
From the conspiracy of men
Will keep them within your secret tent
Far from the strife of plotting tongues
Blessed are you
Who have soothed me with kindness
In the midst of a contentious world
In my despair I cried that I was cut off from you

And you heard my words when they were voiced
You preserve the love and trust of the faithful
And give recompense to the presumptions of the proud

> All you whose hope is in God—
> Be strong and of good cheer

Happy is the one who is forgiven
Whose wound is healed
Happy the one restored to your harmony
In whose spirit there is no more deceit

When I held my silence
My bones grew brittle with crying all day
For by day and night your hand lay heavy on me
And my life's moisture dried up
Through the long droughts of summer

But then I turned toward my mistakes and shortcomings
Knew my unworthiness, did not cover it up
I said, "I will confess all this, since it is so"
And you forgave me for what I am

Therefore let all the faithful
When they find their confusion find you
And pray that the waters of self-delusion
Won't crest to crush them in their time

You are my shelter
You help me withstand my suffering
I endure it warmed in the winds of your exultant songs

I will instruct and I will teach the way to go
I will counsel, my eye is on you

Don't be like a horse or mule
That has no understanding
That must be led along with bridle and bit
His constant ornament
Lest he bump or push or go off course

Many are the pains of the heedless
Those who hold back from you
But the one who trusts self all to you
Will swim in your kindness

So the upright rejoice in you and are glad
The upright in heart shout for joy

UPRIGHT HEARTS rejoice in you
For them praise comes naturally
They play gratefulness on the harp
Pluck it out on the ten-stringed lute
They sing you a new song
Lilted gracefully, irresistibly

For your word is upright
Your works are faithful
Uprightness and justice are the shape of your love
The earth is full of your kindness
The heavens are made of your word
And animated with your breath
You gather together the waters of the sea in heaps
And store them in the vaults of the deep
The earth is awestruck
And all that lives stands openmouthed
For in your speaking the unsayable word
All that is comes to be
Your saying bursts forth
And all holds fast

You reduce the grand schemes of nations to nothing
Bring to less than nothing people's little notions
Your plan stands forever
Your thoughts pierce all the generations

Happy is the nation that loves you
The people who have chosen you
You look out from the center at beings all round
From your place you shine your eye on all that lives
You fashion their hearts
You inspire their deeds

A king is not saved by a mighty army
A strong man is not protected by strength
A horse is useless in the struggle
No, we cannot escape by that power

Your eye is on those who recognize you
Whose hope is in your kindness
That lifts up their souls from death's weight
That brightens their hearts in the dark time

We sit silent, waiting for you
For you are our help, our defense
In you our hearts find their joy
For we trust your unsayableness
Your kindness will stir us like a breeze
That refreshes our body's hope

Every moment I bless you
Your praise is always in my mouth
My soul boasts of you
The humble hear it and rejoice

Join me—let's enlarge God
Let's shout and dance the nameless together
I looked for you and you found me
Delivered me from all that I feared

All who search for you are radiant
Their faces never eclipsed in shame
This poor man cried out and you heard him
Delivered him from his distress

Your angel makes camp
Near those who are brushed by awe
Who taste and see your goodness—
Happy are they who trust you

Holy ones, be awestruck in God
And you'll want nothing more
Young lions crave and go prowling
But those who seek you are satisfied

Come, children, listen to me
I will teach you how to fall back in awe
Who has a passion for life
Loves every day and exults in happiness?

Guard your tongue from crookedness
And your lips from deceit
Avoid evil, do good
Seek peace—pursue it

Your eyes are directed toward them
Your ears lean into their cries
But your anger turns on those who do evil
To cut off its seed from earth's remembering

They cry out and you hear them
And bring them home, back from their distresses
You are close to them in their brokenheartedness
Embracing them in their contrition

The faithful know many sorrows
But in the midst of them you appear and turn them
You hold them as close as their bones
And not one is broken

Pain will snap the crooked
Oppressors will know remorse
But you enliven those who love you
And none who trust you will know remorse

I FEEL THE HEEDLESS IMPULSE in my heart

It speaks to me as to the wicked
Saying, "Pay no attention to God who is before your eyes"

Instead he loves his own eyes
That blind him to desire's poisons
So that he doesn't know enough to seek the good
The words of his mouth are crooked and deceitful
What wisdom's in his heart he fails to notice
What goodness is natural to him he pushes aside
He lies on his bed at night devising schemes
So that in the morning he stumbles down crooked paths
Of suffering but he does not know what he is doing

Your kindness reaches into the darkened center
Your faithfulness all the way up to the empty sky
Your uprightness is like the mountains
Your actions like the sea
Giving birth to all creatures endlessly

How precious is your kindness!
And those who seek your wide wings' shelter—
They will be satisfied with your provisions
They will drink the delights of your streams
For you are life's wellspring
You are the light within the light

Draw down finer the thread of your kindness
For those who recognize you
Draw down the strong filament of your uprightness
For those whose hearts are upright
Don't let the foot of pride be in my step
Or the hand of wickedness be raised up in mine

There they are—those who have lost their way—
Thrust down
Unable to rise

Don't fear the heedless ones
Don't envy those who veer off
For they will be mowed down like the grass
They will wither like the green herb

Trust what is and do good
Be where you are in truthfulness
Take delight in what is
And your heart's desire will be fulfilled

Be committed to life
Trust what is
And all will be as it must be
And your rightness will shine forth as the dawn
And your goodness as the sun at high noon

Be quiet before what is
Wait patiently and simply
Don't worry about those who easily prosper
The manipulators and seducers

Give up anger, give up hatred
Don't think to take revenge or subvert
For the heedless will be cut off

As for those who wait for you—
The world will be theirs to love
Wait only a little while and the heedless ones will be gone
You may look for them in their places but they will not
    be there

The quiet ones will be the world's lovers
Will delight in the fullness of peace

Though the heedless intend harm
Though they lash out tooth and nail
You laugh at them
For you know that their day is at hand

They have drawn the sword and bent the bow
To bring down the needy and destroy the upright
But the sword will pierce their own hearts
And the bow will be snapped in two

Better is the little the upright have
Than the much possessed by the heedless
For their arms will be broken
While you guard the upright
And keep them whole

You are present in the hours of their days
As a constant heritage beyond time
During unhappy seasons they will not be brought low
During famine years they will yet be satisfied

But the heedless will disappear like the beauty of
    meadows
That passes away quickly in smoke
They borrow but do not repay
But the upright are beneficent and give

For those you love will be the world's lovers
And those you dismiss will be cut off

You establish the steps of the upright
And they find pleasure in their lives
Even when they fall they are not downcast
For you lift them up

I have been young and I have grown old
But I have never seen the upright forsaken
Nor their children wanting for bread
They are always beneficent, always gracious
And their children are a blessing to them

Leave off heedlessness, do only good—
Those who make this choice
Abide outside of time
For you love the lovers
You never forsake the lovers
They abide outside of time
But the heedless will be cut off

The upright will be the world's lovers
They will abide in the world outside of time
Their mouths utter wisdom
And their tongues speak what is true
Your endless pattern is in their hearts
And their steps will never falter

The heedless are lurking in the isolated darkness
Seeking the upright, to destroy them
But you will never allow it

Wait, wait with what is
Live in accord with it—
Those who choose this way will be the world's lovers
When the heedless are cut off
They will be there, looking on
I have seen the terrible power of the heedless
Striking deep like the root of a green tree in its native
    land

Yet he disappeared, he was no more
I looked for him but he could not be found

Observe the people of goodness
Behold the upright ones—
Theirs is a happy future
They will know the fullness of peace
But the heedless, the crossers of what is
Those who veer off, fall away, take apart—
They disappear together
Their future is cut off

As for the upright—you are their salvation
Their strength in times of distress
You help them, rescue them, make them whole
Rescue them from heedlessness
Keep them safe
Because they are the ones
Who have trusted you
Who've given themselves wholly over
To waiting with what is

I SAID, I WILL BE CAREFUL
Lest I err with my tongue
I will muzzle my mouth
While in the presence of crookedness

I was dumb, in deep silence
Quite still, restrained
Yet I was in great pain

My heart burned inside me
And in my holding fast
There were flames
And then I spoke

Tell me my end
The measure of my days
What it is—
I want to know
When I will cease to be

You have made me for a shape in time
That has an end, a final day
But to you it is nothing

Yes, as nothing, less than nothing
Does every person stand where he is
Walk about like a shadow, an image

Yes, making a useless noise
Amassing things
Without knowing who will use them in the end

And now—what shall I expect?
I have hope
But it is only for you

Deliver me from my confusion
Don't let me be foolish
I am dumb, I say nothing
Only you speak

Cure this disease you've afflicted me with
I am lashed with your whip

You straighten my crookedness
And all my accomplishments are eaten away in the dark
Like clothing by a moth
A person is no more than a breath

Hear my prayer
Open your ears to my cry
Don't be silent to my tears
For I have wandered unknowing into your presence
As my forebears did

Look away from me for a time
So I can recover my strength
Before I travel on
And am gone

I WAITED PATIENTLY FOR YOU
And you leaned toward me
And heard me
And raised me up from the pit
From the mud, from the clay
And set my foot upon a rock
So that my step was firm
And put a new song on my lips
Your song
That many may hear it with awe
And have confidence in you

Happy is the one who trusts you
And abandons self-pride and deceit
You have done many things
Your wonders, your deeds, your vows—
Nothing can compare to them—
I will sing of them though they are indescribable and
    numberless

You do not need sacrifice and material offerings—
You have opened up my ears to hear it—
That burnt offerings and sin offerings you do not desire

Then I said, Look, I am here
And saw the dark words written on the white page
And my heart's desire became yours
Your law the shape of my heart

I announced it in the Great Assembly
Spoke out my conviction to all
Did not close my lips with it
As you well know
I have never hidden you in my heart for myself

But have spoken openly of your salvation and faithfulness
I have not concealed your kindness and its truth
From the Great Assembly, I have spoken it out freely

>So do not withhold your mercy from me now
>Let your kindness and its truth pour over me
>>continually

For endless trouble surrounds me
My own crooked deeds have overtaken me
I am blind with them
They are more numerous than the hairs on my head
And my courage is gone

Let it be your desire now
To relieve me of this
May all that is in me that caused it
Find a true humility
May all that seeks to dim my soul—
Let all that restlessness come to quiet
Let it be turned around, confounded
May all that says to me, "Aha! Aha!"
Be astonished and humbled
Let it blush with its shame
And may all that seeks for you
Be glad and take delight in you
And may they continually sing of your magnificence
Those who love your ways

Though I am oppressed and needy now
I know you will think of me
My help, my deliverer

>O don't delay!

As the hart thrills for the fresh brook
So do I thrill for you
I am thirsty for you—for my life—
When will I go there?
When will I be seen?
When will I enter your utter presence?

I have swallowed my tears all day and all night
Because people mock me all day saying
"Where is your beloved? Show us, convince us"

When I remember these things
My heart pours out within me:
How I journeyed with the pilgrim throngs
My ears alive with thanksgiving songs
Up to your house for the festival—
Why am I downcast and disturbed?

My hope is yet in you
One day I will thank you
When in you I find wholeness
And my anguish is gone

How my heart is broken, pours out within me!
Therefore I will remember you
From the land of Jordan, from the peaks of Hermon
From the foothills there

Deep calls out to deep
In your towering waterfall
Waves and billows drench me

In the daytime you summon your kindness
And at night you sing to me
A prayer for my life to be living

So I will rise in the morning and sing to you,
My rock, why have you forgotten me?

Why must I walk
Grieving up and down
Oppressed and opposed?
My very bones snap

When the others revile me all day long saying,
"Where is your beloved? Show me, convince me"
Why is my heart broken, pouring out within me?

My hope is yet in you
And one day I will give you thanks
When I am whole

YOU ARE OUR PROTECTION and strength
Help in the storm of anguish and despair
Exactly and easily found close at hand
So we are not afraid

Even when earth's in upheaval
When mountains are carried to the sea
When the sea's waters roar and foam
And the mountains quake and tremble with the waters'
    swelling—

In the middle of the world there is a river
Streams run to it, making glad your cities
Making glad the places where you are known
You flow as the waters of that river
And she shall not be moved
For you are with her
You are the morning that dawns over the quiet waters

Nations rage, kingdoms tumble—
This is the sound of your voice
This is the earth melting away

You are with us, our defense, our silent center
What we see is all your doing
These desolations
These terrifying moments—
Only your unmoving movement—

You cause wars to cease when they cease, to cease forever
You break the bow, snap the spear
Burn up the war wagons

Be still—be still
And know me
Be still and know
That I am what the nations grope toward
I am earth's desire

So we know you are with us
Our defense at the silent center of things

You are greatness
Greatness that is greatly to be sung
In your perfect city
On your holy mountain

The place is loveliness
The whole earth's joy
Mount Zion in the north
Home of the great king
In her inner palaces
You dwell as a silent refuge

For there the kings assemble
They appear and they disappear together
They look and they are astonished
They grieve and they hasten away
Terror seizes them, pain
As a woman giving birth

With the east wind you crush the ships of Tarshish
This I have heard and I have seen it
In your intimate city
Your city established forever

At its center
I have felt your loving-kindness

In your unsayable name
All the songs that cover the earth sing
In your right hand
All that is is made perfect

Let Mount Zion rejoice
Let the daughters of Judah be glad

For what you are
And for what is created by what you are

Compass the mountain round
Walk round and round about her
Count her towers and spires
Hold them in mind and adore them
With your eye take measure of her outer wall
See the inner palaces and chambers
So that you will remember them
And hold them in your heart always

For you are our guide beyond time
Even into death

PEOPLE, LISTEN TO ME
Open your ears, inhabitants of the perishable world
Low and high, rich and needy, all of you—

My mouth will speak wisdom
My heart's speech will be true
I will give myself over to my meaning
Will sing it, play it out on the lyre—

Why should I fear the sorrow
Of being diminished by the honored of the world
Who trust in their wealth
And glory in their riches?

No amount of money can redeem a soul
It cannot be ransomed with gold
For a soul is worth far too much
And if you try to purchase it
It is lost forever

Will the wealthy live endlessly?
Will they buy their way out of the grave?
They are not blind—
They can see that the wise also die
So the fool and the powerful must likewise perish
And leave their wealth to others

Inwardly they imagine
That their legacies will last forever
That their immense houses and estates
Will stand for generations
They even give them their names
In the languages of the countries where they stand

Nevertheless
A person is not an enduring idea
A person perishes, like any animal
Such is the foolish faith of self-confidence
The end of those pleased with their own talk

Like sheep they're herded into death
Who eats them alive at night
And the next morning they find themselves servants of
    the upright
And their substance thins all through the day
And by nightfall they have little left to be proud of

My fate is otherwise—
For you
Will guide my soul
Even in the land of the dead
It won't hurtle there blind—
You will take me

So don't be afraid of the rich
Don't envy the increase of their houses
For when they die none of it matters
When they go down their glory won't follow them
Though they congratulate themselves in their lifetimes
Their souls surfeited with self-satisfaction
They will never see the light again

Because such people make no effort to understand this
They lose their birthright of splendor
And perish, like any animal

You—out of your namelessness—
Spoke
Summoning the world
From the rising to the setting of the sun
Out of Zion, beauty's perfection
You shone forth
Arriving
Breaking the silence
A fire before you
Swirled round with a terrible cloud
Calling out the heavens above
And the earth below
For proving your people

Gather the faithful
Through whose pledge
They are bound together with me

Then the heavens shone forth your justice
And you proved what is

Hear, people, and I will speak—
You who struggle with me
You who question me
I will testify
For I am the is of what is—
Yours that is—

Your sacrifice doesn't appease me
Nor the offerings you dutifully make
I will not take a bullock out of your house
Nor a goat from your fold

All the life of all the forests
All the cattle on a thousand mountains
Is already mine—
I embrace the mountain fowl
Whatever moves in the fields moves in me

If I were hungry, would I come crying to you for food?
I am the world and all that animates it
Do I need to eat the flesh of fatted calves
Or drink the blood of goats?

Offer me your heart's intention
Pay me your forged words
Give me your sorrows—call on me
So I can answer you
So that your soul can speak to me

And to the crooked you said—

Who are you to repeat my words
To mouth my commitments?
You recite but the words don't go in
Instead you throw them down behind you
When you see a thief you congratulate him
Betrayers are your comrades
You flex your mouth with crooked words
Loosen your tongue with deceit
Speak against your brother
Against your own mother's son spew out slander

All this you do ordinarily
Blind to your own actions
And I have kept silence
To see what you would do

And you thought I approved you
Because you cannot think with your own mind
So now I will make it clear
So that it is set in order before your eyes
Think about it
Think about your heedlessness
And do it soon
Before the backlash of your deeds
Tears you to pieces
And even I cannot help you—

Who offers me his heart's intention
Brightens me, extends me
Who turns his course around
Will feel my kindness and my help

BE GRACIOUS WITH ME in your loving-kindness
In your tenderness blot out my confusion
Wash me, let my impurity run off
Cleanse me, squeeze the poison out
For of my twistedness I'm painfully aware
My weakness is before my eyes all day long

Against you, weaver of the hidden pattern of things
Has the shape of my actions inclined
Necessarily—
For I am human
And my pain must rend the cloth
Unraveling right and wrong
Tearing the fabric of my own heart
That in its woundedness it has no choice but to seek for
     you

From the first I was this way
Mothered in conception and division—
Your eye looks through the fabric to the nothing
     beyond—
Cause me there, in my soul's exile, to find brightness
Freshen me with hyssop
Wash my heart and my body will be whiter than snow
Let me hear with the inward ear the gladness and the
     joy
Of my sensual life
So that the bones you've crushed in bringing me to be
Can click and sing, repaired
Let the light of your eye in mine
Clarify my tangles and snarls
So they do not pull nor strangle
And my heart becomes clear
And my spirit new

Don't push me away
Don't remove your natural love
Remind me of the joy I find in immersion in you
Support me—free me—
And I will remember you to all who've fallen away
And they'll rise up, face to face with you again
Deliver me from division within myself
That I can find my tongue to sing your allness—
Open my lips and my mouth will praise you
For this is what you desire, not sacrifice

If you wanted burnt offerings I'd give them
But the sacrifice you desire is a broken heart
A humbled heart, quiet and receptive
You will always receive
Take it and make Zion strong
Take it and pile high the walls of Jerusalem
And then the rites and rituals will make sense
Then the bullocks and the incense can be offered on
    the altars

LISTEN TO MY PRAYER
Don't hide from my petition
Listen and respond

I am tossed about, moaning
Deafened by the clamor of the wicked
Pressed down by the weight of the heedless
Who bring down their darkness upon me
And prick me on all sides with their restless fury

My heart convulses
Death's terror invades
Fear and trembling rattle my bones
My whole body shudders

I said, O that someone
Would give me the wings of a dove
I would fly away from here to a quiet place
I would lie down in the evening in the wilderness
I would find shelter from the punishing wind
And from the storm

Confuse their speech!
For I have seen violence and strife in the city
Day and night they surround her walls
And inside there is confusion and meanness
Hatred gathers in the square
Deceit and twistedness growl in the streets

It is not an enemy who bests me—
            I could bear that
Not one who hates me and grows large with hatred—
            Against him I would know how to hide

No, it is someone close, warm, intimate
My friend and my guide
With whom I walked arm and arm in your house
In sweet fellowship—

Whose heart is divided
Enters death alive
Living in the shadows of disjunction
I call on you
Knowing you will make me whole

In the evening and the morning and at noon
I moan and shout out my anguish
And I am heard
Delivered by you unharmed
From these endless battles

In you I have thousands by my side
You who occupy the sovereign throne
Since time's beginning
Hear me
And pull them down—
Those who do not recognize the power of change
And so forget you
Who betray friends, who break trust
Whose creamy words flow smoothly from the mouth
But whose heart hates
Whose words soothe like oil
Yet they are drawn swords

I entrust myself wholly to you—
You hold me up
You never let the upright collapse

But you will bring them down—
Those of blood, those of the lie
The partial ones will not live out half their days

My trust is yours

BE GRACIOUS, BE GRACIOUS, be gracious
For my soul flies out to your protection
Flies up to the refuge of your wings
Until this anguish passes

I call on you, my guide
Confident of your kindness to me
You who swirls out from the center
And penetrates me with your love
Though the one who wants to swallow me up
Utters curses and accusations
Your faithfulness will still them all

I am in the company of lions by day
At night I lie down in flames
Their teeth are spears and arrows
Their tongues a sharpened blade

> *Raise yourself up and blaze out over all the body*
> *of earth!*

They prepared a net to ensnare my foot—
      I was almost caught
They dug a pit for me—
      But they fell into it

My heart is firm, my heart is firm, my heart is firm
I sing it, I chant it, I pluck it on the lyre
Awake, my soul!
Awake, harp and psaltery!
I will wake up the dawn with my song!
I will go out among the people with my chanting!
I will rouse the nations with my playing!

For your kindness swirls about the entire center
And your truth reaches as far as the empty sky

> Raise yourself up and blaze out over all the body
>   of earth!

RELEASE ME FROM TORMENT
Defend me against opposition
Relieve me of crookedness
From blood hate let me be free

Look: they lie in wait for my soul
Mighty, they gather in troops against me
Not because of my transgressions
Not because of my shoddy deeds
For no reason I know
They rush to prepare an attack—

Rouse yourself, wake up the defenses!
Come near me and see
You, protector of the strugglers
Awaken and overturn the enemies
Show them mercy by giving them their due

They will return in the evening
Howling like dogs
Prowling round the city streets
Sputtering, raving with their mouths
Swords clashing within their lips
They say, Who hears us?

But you laugh at them
You hold them all in derision

Because he is fierce
I wait for you—
You are my only defense

You are kindness
You go before me

Letting me see
The shape of my hope
Against this torment
No matter how strong

O don't destroy them
Then I would forget
But drive them upward
And bring them to rest

You my shield, my barrier
Because of their misdirected mouths
The confusion of their lips
Let them be caught by their pride
By the lies and accusations they utter
Let their fury finally end
Let it be no more
And let them know at last
That you are Jacob's mystery
As far and as wide as the earth is

And they will return in the evening
Howling like dogs
Prowling round the city streets
Mad for something to eat
Lunatic for satisfaction
Lusting for something to bring them peace

But I—
I sing of your strength
Yes, in the morning's dawn
I sing the steadying light of your kindness
For you have been my release

My refuge on a day when I was full of distress
To you my strength will I sing
For you are my shield
My kindness

My soul waits quietly for you
From you comes my deliverance
Only you are my rock my redemption
My haven: I shall not be moved

How long will they press on me
Push on me as though I were a leaning wall
A tottering fence?

Whenever I rise up
They pull me down
Delighting in deception
Blessing with their mouths
But cursing in their hearts

Yes, wait quietly my soul
For you only do I hope in silence
Only you are my rock, my deliverance
My haven: I shall not be moved

You are my completion, my brightness
You my strength, my protection

Let us trust you always
Pouring out our hearts to you
Our refuge, our solace

To be human is nothing
To be great is a lie
Heaped up on the scale
They rise up in the balance
For altogether they are lighter than nothing

Don't rely on deception
Or put your hope in robbery
Even if they bring you prosperity
It will do no good

You spoke once
And you spoke again
What I have heard:

That strength is built on you
That kindness flows from you
That you are the certain recompense
For all according to their acts

FOR YOU PRAISE WAITS in Zion
Vows pile up to be paid
All that lives readies to advance
To you who hears these words

I am weary of the world's crookedness
And my own confusions—
You will straighten and correct it
With forgiveness wiping woes away

Happy are those you choose
Who approach you and dwell in your house
Who are satisfied with that happiness
The holiness of your house

Terrific deeds of rightness are your answer to our
      words
You who are the confidence of rock and sea
The faithfulness of mountains
Their might and majesty
Who guides the roaring of the seas
The pounding of the towering waves
The tumultuous fortunes of nations

Those who dwell in the outermost lands
Are awed by your daily wonders
The dawning of the morning
And the fading of the evening
They rejoice in as your body's calling

Your thought of earth
Is the gathering of her waters
The enriching of her soils
Your brook runs with water

And so you prepare the harvest
That feeds life

Saturating her furrows
Smoothing her ridges
Softening her with showers
Murmuring the blessings
Of her growing

Your crown is the ample unfolding of the years
Your body the presence in physical places
The pastures of the wilderness distill it
The hills of the settlements disperse its joy
The meadows are clothed with flocks
The valleys mantled with grain
The people give voice to it with words
They murmur it, shout it, sing it out

ENDOW POWER WITH JUSTICE
Let it embrace uprightness
So that people can see uprightness before them
And the downtrodden can be raised up in justice

Let the mountains hold peace fast for people
Let the hills reverberate with the movements of justice
Give power eyes to see the needy
So that it can serve them and their children
Crushing what holds them down

And all will respect you as long as the sun will shine
As long as the moon will glow in the night sky
For all the generations to come

Let power be for refreshment
Like rain upon mown grasses
Like showers on the open earth
Let it cause uprightness to grow lush
Let it make peace spring up in abundance
Till the moon falls out of the sky

And you will have dominion from sea to sea
From the river to the far end of the land
Before you all those yet wild will bow
And the enemies will lick the dust

The kings of Tarshish and of the isles will bring gifts
The kings of Sheba and Seba will likewise arrive with
    offerings
Even all the kings will bow before you
And all the nations will recognize you

For you respond to the needy when they cry out
To the sufferer when there is no hope
You care for the poor and the broken
You soothe their souls
Plucking out the barbs of crookedness and violence
Their lifeblood is precious to you
And they will live and you will give them Sheba's gold
And will pray on their behalf constantly
Blessing them all the time

There will be grain in abundance in the land
To the tops of the mountains the sheaves will tremble
Rattling with fullness like the treetops of Lebanon
And people will blossom out of the cities
Like wild herbs spreading over the fields

Your name will flourish
People will bless themselves with your memory
Nations will understand happiness when they think of
    you

For you are blessedness
You who give strength to the strugglers
Who answer the questioners
Who alone animate wonders
Your unsayable name is glorious
It fills the world to the brim with its brightness

IT IS TRUE—THE STRUGGLERS
Find the good through you
When they find a pure heart

But as for me
I am easily unbalanced
Easily do I slip and almost fall
I am envious of the high and mighty
Desire the prosperity of the wicked
They do not seem to have mortal fears
Their strength seems self-sufficient
They seem to escape their human weakness
And they don't bother with the worries of others
They wear pride for a necklace
Violence for a cloak
Their eyes stare out from fattened cheeks
For they've consumed more than any heart could
desire
They dissemble, they speak out against oppression
Loftily do they speak
With their mouths fastened onto heaven
While their tongues run craftily about the earth
And when the thirsty return from their long journeys
The cup is dry for they have drained it
And they say with impunity
No one sees us, no one knows what we are
For the lofty God to whom we pray is far removed from
here

Yes, these are the wicked
This is how they are
Yet daily they increase in wealth
And there seems no end to their successes

Why have I piously cleansed my heart?
Why have I bothered to wash these hands in innocence
Working all day to be pure
Waking up every morning aware of my shortcomings?
I am disgusted with it all
But if I dare speak of it
I betray my creed and fellows
Even to think of it
Would do damage to my own eyes

But then
I entered your house
And now I understand truly
How it is with the wicked

They are on high and the place is firm
But the spot is slippery
And in the darkness they find no step
And surely will they fall to their end in nothingness
In every moment
They perish desolately, meet themselves drastically
With terrific events
When you wake from your dream of them
Their outward selves even fade in the light of day

Before, my heart soured with anger
And I felt the bite of the reins of my envy
But I was foolish, unable to see
Your truth was spoken before me
Yet like an animal
I could not understand the words
Though my ears heard the sound

Now
I know
I am continually
With you
You have taken
My right hand
And led me quiet
Into your house
Guided me
With daily
Awareness of you
And when my life ends
You will take me again
Into the limitless fire
That has always burned in me

What use is heaven?
And on earth I need nothing
Save you

Though my flesh and my heart shall fail
Yet my heart's foundation
Does not come or go
Those who live far from you
Have already perished in that—
Your absence
Is their punishment
It is already done

     But as for me
     I draw nearer you always
     And it is good
     My trust is in knowing you
     In speaking only of what you are

WHY HAVE YOU CAST US off forever?
Why does your anger smoke at the flock you tend?
Remember us, yours for so long
Your image, your inheritance, closer to you than yourself
This Zion where your presence dwells

Lift up your feet
Walk onto these endless ruins
Hatred and division have wrecked your sanctuary
Violence has roared into the midst of the peaceful
    assembly

They've mistaken their signs for signs
Turning the world upside down
They've lifted up axes against the forests
Hacked away at your handiwork with hatchets and
    hammers
Set fire to your sanctuary
Burned to the ground
The dwelling place of your unsayableness

They have said in their hearts
We will oppress them altogether
They have burned up every place that is yours
No part of the land is untouched by them
So we can no longer see signs
And we cannot speak truth
And no one knows how long we will suffer this

How long
Will the adversary
Speak lies?
Will division
Forever ignore

Your unsayableness?
Why withdraw your hand
Your right hand?
Draw it out—
Act

You are our ruler
From times of old
Working out salvation
Here on the land

By your strength
You divided the sea
Broke into pieces
The beasts of the deep
Crushed Leviathan's heads
And fed them to the people
Of the wilderness
And so made the world

You cracked open
Springs and torrents
Pushed back
Flooding rivers
You are the day
You are the night
Hauled up to the sky
The sun's blaze
Tapped out the rhythm
Summer and winter
You breathed them

Don't forget this:
That they've defiled you

That the foolish ones have trampled your unsayableness
Don't give us up to the many heedless ones!
Don't forget forever the congregation of the afflicted
    ones!

Don't forget your promise
For in the shadows of the world violence thrives
Don't send the oppressed back dismayed
Give the poor and needy good reason to praise you

Arise
Plead your own cause
Keep the memory of their defiance in your mind
Hear their voices in your ear
Their snarling noises ascending all the time

WE GIVE THANKS TO YOU, endless thanks
For the nearness of your unsayableness
That we touch in the memory of your wondrous doing

For I will when the right time comes
Make right judgment—
The earth and all living things melt away
It is I who keep the pillars firm

I say to the arrogant, let go of arrogance
And to the crooked, put down your horns—
Put them down, all the way down
And lower your proud stiff necks
For what truly lifts
Comes neither from the rising of the sun
Nor from the setting of the sun
Nor from the wild power of desert mountains
But only from me
Who when that time comes
Lowers one
And lifts another
I hold the cup in my hands
And the whipped wine foams
That I pour off clearly
But the sour dregs they drain—
This is the drink of the crooked

I will endless sing a hymn to you
Who hack off the horns of the crooked
But the horns of the upright you raise

I SHOUT OUT TO YOU, I wail—
Give me your ear
In the day of my torment my eyes seek you
In the night of my despair my hands ceaselessly grope
My soul refuses to be comforted
I think of you and moan
I think of my life and my spirit is crushed
You keep my eyes from shutting
Until I am overcome and cannot speak
Remembering times gone by
Years of the past, repressed deeds
I sing ancestral songs
Communing with my heart
Inquiring acutely within my spirit

Will you cast me off forever?
Will I never gain your favor again?
Is your kindness depleted
Your promise dried up for all time?
Have you forgotten how to pity
Walled off with anger your compassion?

And I said, No—
It's my own infirmity
My own withholding
That stays your hand

Against this will I recall your doing, contemplate your
    being
You whose path is holiness—
Where is there goodness to compare with yours?
You, architect of wonders
You, author of strength
Who saved the struggling, the captured, people

The waters saw you and were convulsed
To their depths they shuddered
The clouds threw off water
The skies rumbled
Lightning arrows shot zigzag across the sky
As the wheeling whirlwind voiced out thunder
And lightning flashed the world to shocked view—
The whole earth churned and rolled

Your way cut a path through the seas
A path through mighty waters
But your tracks could not be seen
You led us like a flock
In Moses and Aaron's care

LISTEN, SHEPHERD OF ISRAEL

You who lead us like a flock
You who live distant surrounded by angels—
Shine forth! Don't hold back your light!
Before Ephraim and Benjamin and Menassah
Awaken your power and help us!

Turn our hearts around, shine on us, open us up

How long will your anger smoke against our prayers?
How long will you feed us with the bread of tears
Tease our thirst with the water of tears in endless
    measure?
You set our neighbor against us
Make us a laughingstock—

Turn our hearts around, shine on us, open us up

You took a vine cutting out of Egypt
Plucked out the choking weeds and planted it
Cleared the ground and it struck root
Spreading out over all the land
Till its shadow covered the mountains
Its boughs hung out over the mighty cedars
It sent out tendrils all the way to the sea
Its shoots entered the rivers

Why have you now broken down the fences
So that passersby pluck its fruit
Wild boars gnaw at it
And the furtive creatures of the field
Feed on it mercilessly in the night?

Come back to us, look down from your heights—
Think of this vine
Of the stock planted with your right hand
The root that you yourself made strong

It is scorched by fire, hacked down
Withered because you turned aside your face

Reach down to the people at your right hand
To the ones whom you've forged to be your agent
We will not veer off from you
Revive us so we can call out your unsayableness

Turn our hearts around, shine on us, open us up

.

I SING TO YOU MY STRENGTH
My joy I also sing
Chanting a psalm, tapping a drum
The pleasant harp and the psaltery

At the new moon I blow the trumpet
On the feast day, the appointed day
For this is the way you've set forth
As a law and as an ordinance
As witness in Joseph you invoked it
When he went out over Egypt, that narrowness
And heard a language never heard before
When you removed the burden from his shoulder
And freed his hands from the carrying baskets

All this I do but is it enough?

You called me in distress and I answered you
I answered you in the secret of the thunder
And proved you in the waters of the wilderness
So now I can say to you:

Hear this warning
O you who would rise up to struggle and question—
Listen to me!

Do not give yourself to what's limited
Do not strip your soul of its immensity
For I have brought you into the clearing
Out into the open
Out from your narrowness and dimness

Open wide your mouth
And I will fill it up with song

From me the melody unlimited
And from no other thing

But you do not hear this saying of mine
There is no willingness in you
To follow the way I ordain and uphold
The way I speak with my everywhere-clear voice

So I let you go on in your cramped blindness
Left you to your wandering minds and foolish devices
Your hearts frozen, I let you take your own counsel

> *I regret it!*
> *I ought to have shouted to you: Follow me!*

And if you had heard me
All opposition would revolve toward harmony
All the world would bend to the good
And time would be free of itself
And the finest wheat would endless grow
And out of the rock sweet honey would flow

How LOVELY IS YOUR HOUSE!

My soul thirsts for, longs for your courts

My heart and my flesh leap for joy

In your presence, life's sovereignty

Just as the sparrow has found her proper nest

And the swallow a corner for herself

Where she may nurture and fledge her young

So have I found your altars

You who trail clouds of glory

To whom I look for my soul's satisfaction

Happy are they who live in your house

Their lives are your continuous praise

Happy the ones whose hearts confide in you

Whose feet walk the pilgrim pathways

Passing the valley of weeping

They change it into a spring

And the morning rains cover it with blessing

They go from strength to strength, tower to tower

Appearing before you at Zion's Mount

O you who trail clouds of glory—

Listen to me, incline your ear

And look upon my glistening face

For better is a day in your courts

Than a thousand days anywhere else

I would rather wait at the threshold of your house

Than dwell comfortable in the tents of the strong

For you are a warm sun, a glinting shield

Who beams grace, who shines glory

Never withholding goodness

From those who walk with integrity—

O you whose glory blazes behind you!

Happy is the one whose trust rests solid with you

Psalm 84

LISTEN TO ME, ANSWER ME, for I am desperate
Protect my soul, for I am steadfast
O you to whom I am ever calling
In whom I am always trusting
Help me now
Be gracious with me
I call out to you all day long
Let my soul rejoice with relief
For I lift it up to you who are good, forgiving
Abundant in kindness to all who call out to you
Listen to my prayer, hear my desperation's voice
On the day of my distress I call on you
Knowing you will answer
You the incomparable one
Whose deeds are inconceivable

All the nations you have made
Will come to bow before you
Honoring your unsayable name
For you are boundless greatness
And your deeds are wonders, inexplicable
There is only you, you alone

Teach me your path
And I will walk firmly in your truth
Let my heart be undivided in awe of your namelessness
And I will thank you with all my heart
And will honor your unsayableness forever
For your kindness toward me is great
You have saved my soul from the deep

Arrogant ones have risen against me
Ruthless ones seek my life
These are the ones who do not see you

But you are full of mercy
Gracious and kind
Slow to anger, steadfast in love and truth

O turn to me
Be gracious with me
Give me your strength
Save the child of your maidservant
Fix me with a sign of goodness
So those who oppose me can see it and be ashamed
Knowing you have helped me and given me comfort

You love Zion's gates
Built by you on holy mountains
More than all the dwellings of Jacob

Glorious things are spoken here
O place of wholeness—
I'll mention Rehab and Babylon

Even these know me
Here is Philistia and Tyre and Ethiopia—
We too were born here

Indeed of Zion it will be said
Everyone was born here
And here wholeness establishes itself

When I write down the names of peoples
In the final register of all that is
About each of them it will be inscribed

These were born here
Singers and musicians and dancers dwell here
Here is the source of all my joy

Now YOU ARE my only help

By day I cry out to your distances
And at night I stand naked before you
May my prayer touch you
Incline your ear to it, hear me

For my soul is heavy with trouble
And my life is a living death
I am as those who've run out of time
Without vigor, afloat among the dead
Like a murdered corpse, forgotten and denied
Cut off in prime by your hand

You have lowered me to the bottom
Where it is darkest, the deepest dark
You pummel me with your fury
Pound me with your waves

You've driven away all my companions
Made me seem poisonous to them
I am imprisoned, bound, I cannot move

My eyes burn with acid sufferings
And every day I call out to you
Every day I reach out my hands toward you

Will you perform miracles for the dead?
Will the departed ones stand up and offer thanks to you?
Will they open their mouths to speak of your kindness?
Can your miracles be seen in this darkness?
Can your goodness be remembered
Here in the land of endless forgetting?

Yet I cry out more loudly more persistently to you
And in the morning I offer up again my prayer
Why do you throw my soul away?
Why do you hide your face from me?

All my life I am eaten by time
Full of affliction, perishing
I have borne your terrors
Till my mind is distracted

The fire of your anger
Passes over my body
Your terrors have been
My constant devastation
Swirling always about me
I am bathed in them
Pulled down to the bottom
Gasping for breath

You've driven away all my companions
The light in the eye of my lover, my friend
Is altogether put out

I WILL FOREVER SING of your kindness
Throughout the generations with my words I'll make it
    known
For I have pledged, Endless is your kindness
    confirmed
Even in the heavens is your faithfulness patterned

> *I have made a covenant with the one I have
>   chosen*
> *Have sworn to David, my servant, that I will
>   confirm him forever*
> *Will hold up his throne throughout the
>   generations*

And the heavens are the praise of your wonders
Your faithfulness shakes the hallways of the holy ones
For where in the skies can your measure be found?
And who is like you even among all the powers that be?
The hallways of the powerful shrink before your presence
And all greatness trembles before the mention of your
    name
Whose power can compare with your endlessness
That is wreathed all round with steadfast kindness?

You rule the seas—when the waves come rushing
    upward you calm them
You crush original chaos as if it were a weak figment
You scatter the opposing forces and smooth life's way
The heavens pulse with your spirit
The earth rolls on with your thought
As for the world and all that fills it—you stand within it all
North and south: you alone
Tabor and Hermon: your jubilant song

Yours is the powerful arm, the strong hand, exalted is
    your right hand

Your throne's foundation is uprightness and justice
The air around it swirls with clouds of kindness and truth
Happy are those who hear the joyful trumpet blasts
For they'll walk always firm in the light around your face
And they'll be glad all day, soothed by the melody of
    your name's silent syllables
And in your uprightness will they continuously exalt

For you are the glory of our strength
And through your favor are we exalted
For you are our shield and our sovereign—

Then you spoke to me in a vision and said:

> *I have aligned myself with a worthy one*
> *Have raised up a youth from out of the heart of*
>   *the people*
> *I have found David my servant there*
> *And have consecrated him, pouring over his*
>   *head my holy oil*
> *With whom my hand will be firmly*
>   *established*
> *And my arm will give him strength*
> *The enemy won't gouge him like a crooked dealer*
> *Nor will the unjust ones overpower him*
> *For I will push aside from him his assailants*
> *And those that block his way I'll plague*
> *He will always know my steadfast kindness*
> *And through my namelessness will his horn be*
>   *exalted*

And I will place his hand upon the sea
His upright hand upon the rivers
And he will call out to me as his father, his rock,
    his deliverance
Him will I appoint sovereign
For him will I maintain my kindness forever
My covenant with him forever
And forever his forebears and his throne, as long
    as the heavens last

But if his children ignore my pathways
If they walk away from me in willful
    directions
If they subvert my determinations and
    misapprehend my mind
Then I will visit their ignorance with
    suffering
Their self-centeredness I will crack with despair
But I will never excise my forbearing
    kindness from him
I will never betray this commitment I now make
Will never go back on these words of my lips
For I have sworn by my power once and for all
That I will never be false to him
His seed will endure endlessly, his throne like
    the sun before me
Like the moon established forever
A faithful witness in the sky

Yes, but now you have rejected, spurned, despised,
    crushed
Have become enraged at me your anointed one
You have voided your vaunted commitment

Have dragged down that lofty crown into the filth and dust
You've broken all my fences, shattered my protecting
    walls—
All who pass plunder me—I have become an
    embarrassment to my neighbors—
You've lifted up the right hand of my tormentors
And made all my enemies rejoice
Turned back the blade of my sword
And I'm bowed down in battle
My brilliance is darkened, my throne lies cracked on
    the ground
You've cut off my hopeful youthful days
Covered them with a sheath of shame

How long will you continually hide yourself from me?
How long will your anger singe me like fire?
Remember what I am: a feeble person, of brief life and
    quick death—
For what have I been created?
Who can live and not see death daily approaching?
Who can save himself from the dark depth's triumph?
Where is the kindness you swore to me in the
    magnificence of your truth?

Remember now the hardship of your servant
The suffering I bear in my heart
Because of the abusers around me on every side
Remember that these enemies have defiled your purpose
Have caused to fumble the footsteps of your anointed
At every turn of the way

        You who are nonetheless blessed forever—
        In gratitude I speak these words to you

You have always been a refuge to me
Before the mountains, before the earth, before the world
From endlessness to endlessness
You are

You turn me around
You say
Return child

A thousand years to you are like a yesterday
Like a lonely hour in the middle of the night

You rush them away like a flood
Like a long sleep
Like grass
That rises up fresh in the morning
And in the evening withers

I am consumed by you
Terrified by time
And my despair is all too clear
In the light of your face

All my days pass
In your midst
All my years reverberate
Like a solemnly spoken word

The years of our life number seventy
If we are uncommonly strong maybe eighty
Yet they only bring trouble and sorrow
For we can't forget how soon they pass
How swiftly they fly by

Who knows your power?

I can only fear it in the darkness of every night

Help me understand how to count my days
How to embrace my life
That I may nourish a heart of wisdom

Turning around: how long, O Lord, how long!

Think of me
Satisfy me in the morning with your kindness
And I will rejoice all day long

Give me as many days of joy in you
As the days of my natural suffering
The days of my longing and my sorrow

Show me how
You live in me

Bless my children
Light my path with your beauty
So that all that I do will be inspired

Yes,
Establish my life in you
And let all that I do

Be yours

IT IS GOOD TO THANK YOU, good to pronounce your
    unsayable name
With morning's light to remember your kindness
With night's sky to think of your faithful heart
To sing of it with music of the ten-stringed instrument
With the psaltery, with the harp

Because you are at work in what is I rejoice
And the physical world your hands have made
Animates in my body your preciousness

Everything you have made firm is very great
Everything you have coaxed into thought profound
And only someone humane knows this, a fool cannot
    see it

When the crooked spring up like weeds
When the heedless like grasses seem to flourish
It is only so that they may be mowed down

But you
Who do not rise up
And cannot be mowed down
Uplift
What opposes you
And it falls and withers
Scatters and is cast away

Knowing this
My resolve is strengthened
Like a ram's horn freshly anointed it glistens
So that my eyes see clearly the greed of those who envy
And my ears hear patiently the confused cacophony of
    the world

Those who go in accord with you grow fresh as palm
      trees
Grow tall as the cedars of Lebanon
For they are planted in your house, their leaves rustle
      in your courtyards
Even in old age they'll flourish, vigorous and covered
      with foliage
Emblems of your uprightness, your rocklike
      steadfastness
Sealed and without a crack

YOU ARE SOVEREIGN
Clothed with goodness
Dressed in strength

And so the world is firmly established
And it cannot be moved

You, addressed by the world's voice
Are firmly established from the first
And before and after the first

The rivers have been lifted
The rivers' cries, the rivers' shouts have been lifted
The rivers have lifted their dark waves

But more than the thunder of the waters
More than the thumping of the seas
Is you

Your witnessing is steadfast
Your house is ever whole

Even past the end of time

SHINE YOUR LIGHT ON ACTION
O shine your light

Dawn, rise up, illuminate, make clear
Brighten for the eye of the heedless
The darkness of their conduct
The effluent consequence of what they do

How long shall they exult?
How long shall their speech sputter noisily
Words that clash in the ear?

The evildoers in their ignorant confidence
Crush your people
Afflict your heritage

The widow and the stranger they slay
The parentless child they murder
Saying, No one will stop us
For no one sees this
God is too lofty to take notice of it

Take notice you heedless ones!
You doers of thoughtless cruelty
You who mistake your own humanness—

Understand:
When will you wake up?

Do you think that the one who is the hearing of the ear
Does not hear?
Do you think that the one who is the seeing of the eye
Does not see?

Do you think that the one who is profound goodness
Abandons goodness, the brightness of the heart?

And you
Who are our center:
You are the knowing of our endlessness
Awareness of our nothingness
Beyond recognition and name

Who rests in you
Who follows your way
Whose heart is lit with your brightness
Is happy

This one is peaceful in the evil times
Knowing that all deeds fashioned in darkness
Will be lit by your light one day

Knowing that you cannot forsake your people
For we are your heritage
And justice will return to justice—
The upright heart understands this

Where will I find light
In the darkness of my time?

Who will rise up for me
When crookedness lays me low?

Were you not the living center of things
I'd fall back into numb silence

When I feel no ground beneath me
When my foot gives way
Your kindness sustains me

When my painful thoughts collide in confusion
Your quietness is my stability

Can you sustain injustice
Support crooked arrangements made for the powerful?
They band together to twist your law
The holders of power diminish the good
Condemn the innocent, throw aside the weak

But you are ever my comfort
My sheltering rock
Bringing justice to justice
Evil to evil, each act according to its character

Brought home
Brought to wholeness in its time

WE ARE HERE
Singing to you
Erupting into shouting
At the place of the rock of our salvation
Coming gratefully and gracefully before you here
Affirming with our words, the music of our mouths
That we are possessed by you, yours entirely

For you give us the gift of sovereignty
A power above all others
The majesty of our absolutely being

You whose hands touch the earth's depths
Whose heart pierces the mountain peak

The always changing sea is yours for it exists because of
    you
And your hands have formed the firmness of the lands

So we come in awe, offering the earth and sea of
    ourselves to you
Bending what we are toward you, shaper of us

For you are our beyond and we are your doing
Sheep who graze in your pastures, animated by your hand
If only we could awaken to it!

Don't lose heart as you did in the wilderness
When entanglements confused you
In the days when your ancestors lost faith
Demanding outward signs although what is
       —Utter presence—
Was clear

For forty years I was bitter against them and said
"They are a crooked people, blind to what is"
And I then vowed in my anger
That they would never enter my place.

I SING A NEW SONG to you and the earth sings too
I sing and my song blesses your unsayable name
Day by day announcing the utter presence of things
Day by day evoking your glory among the nations
Calling forth your miracles among all the peoples—

You are each place and each thing
And nowhere and nothing
No praise and all praise
No word and all words
Touch this

For it is beyond what can be seen and known—
          —Inconceivable—
You of the eyeless heaven

Grandeur and majesty surround you
Who are scored and marked with light—

Everyone listen!

Recognize this light and this power
Bathe your face in the luminous circle of its named
    namelessness
Place your body there, making of it a gift—

I offer you this life
In the beauty of the dappled world
Trembling before you
Earth's utter presence
Saying fearlessly aloud among the nations:
God alone gives sovereignty
And the world is unshakable
Existence is just

Let the heavens rejoice
Let the earth dance
Let the sea churn with all the life that's in it
Let the fields burst with plenty
And the trees of the forest brim with dignity
In song to you who comes with justice
Who comes with the sweetness of truth

You are sovereign!
The earth is glad
And the islands rejoice

Clouds and thick darkness envelop you
Uprightness and justice support your throne

A fire precedes you
Burning before you all that resists you

Your lightning flashes through the world
The earth is convulsed at the sight
Mountains melt like wax at your presence
At the presence of the sovereign of the earth

The heavens speaking is your rightness
People's seeing is your brightness
All who see something less
And boast of this limited sight
And think it is sufficient
Shall be ashamed one day
When they see that all is nothing but you

Zion, hearing this, rejoices
And glad are the daughters of Judah
Because of what you are and do decree

For you are sovereign over all the earth
Among the holy most holy

All those who love you cast off crookedness
You guard the soul's goodness
Guide it through difficulty
And bring it safely home

Light shines on the upright
Radiance on the goodhearted
The upright rejoice in you
And give thanks for the holiness of memory

To you we sing a new song
For you are full of wonders
Your right hand
Your holy arm
Has been victorious!

You have made your salvation clear
Before the eyes of all
Your rightness is revealed

You remember your kindness and faithfulness
To those who struggle and question
To the ends of the earth
Your salvation is revealed

From all the far-flung lands
A shout is raised up
It breaks forth into song
It erupts into praise

We pluck your praise on the lyre
On the lyre with melodious song
From trumpet and cornet
A blast bursts out
For you, our king

Let the sea and all within it thunder
The world and all of life
Let rivers clap their hands
And mountains kick their heels
At your presence

For you are coming
To awaken all
To establish justice and harmony everywhere

ALL THE EARTH SHOUTS FOR YOU!
We serve you joyfully
Come into your presence
With thanksgiving songs

We know you intimate as all
Know we come from you
Are you
Your people, flock of your pasture, wholly yours

As we enter your gate with thanksgiving songs
Enter your court with chants of praise
We offer all our thanks
And heap blessings on your unsayableness

For you are goodness
Endless kindness
Truthfulness now
And throughout the generations

**Psalm
100**

HEAR MY PRAYER
Let my cry come before you
Don't hide your face from me now
When suffering overwhelms me
Bend your ear toward my wailing
And answer me swiftly

Psalm 102

The days of my life have gone up in smoke
My bones are smoldering like hearth fire logs
And my heart is as dry as desert grass
I can't eat—my groaning bones chatter inside my flesh
I am like a scavenger bird in the wilderness
Like an owl amid the ruins
All hungry eye like a lone bird on a nighttime rooftop

All day long I choke myself with disgust
My own name has become a curse to me
I eat ashes for bread
My drink is soured by my tears
Because of your indignation and wrath—
You who lifted me up
Have thrown me down
My days are like a lengthening shadow
Like the grass I wither and fall back

But you
Sit enthroned
Forever
Your memory
Inspired
Throughout the generations
You will arise
Will lift up Zion

For it is her time
Zion's time is now

Her servants hold dear her stones
Even her dust they cherish
The nations will hold you in awe
The rulers of the world will honor your glory
When you strengthen the soul's Zion
Your light will blaze forth
When you wrap yourself
In the prayer of the forsaken
When you lift that prayer up

This that I say will be written down
For a coming generation
So that those not yet born
Will know how to praise your unsayable name
That you looked down from the center
Opened out the bud of your eye
Full into the world
To bear the sighing of the desperate
To loosen up the binding of death
That the dwellers in Zion can sing out your name
That all Jerusalem can dance your praise
Gathered together in harmony in your service

Yes you weakened me on the journey
Yes you shortened my days
But still I say Do not take me away
In the midst of my life
You whose years go on throughout the generations
In times gone by you made the earth's foundations
The heavens are your handiwork
Even all this will perish

But you will not perish
Yes—all will wear out like a garment
And you will change clothing
The world will be changed like clothing
But you will not change
And your years will know no limit

The children of those who serve you
Will live in the light of this presence
And their seed will be firmly planted
In the soil of this spirit

My soul is for your blessing
All that is within me
A blessing for your nameless holiness
My soul is for your blessing
And remembers your gifts

Who forgives everything
Who heals all diseases
Who redeems life from death
Who makes a sovereign crown
Of kindness and mercy
Who awakens the spirit
So that time's refreshed
And grows back like an eagle's feather
Who brings justice to the unfairly treated
Who makes known your ways to Moses our teacher
And acts in the lives of the strugglers
Who is kind, who is gracious
Steadfast and faithful
Who doesn't contend forever
But lets anger slip away
Whose gifts are gracious and fortuitous
Whose generosity is blind to our shortcomings—

As high as heaven is above the earth
So far, so wide is your kindness to us who seek to know
    you
As far as east is from west
So far, so distant have you removed us from our
    limitations

As a parent loves a child
Freely and unsurpassingly
So have you loved us

For you know who we are
You remember we are dust
Our days like grass
We bloom like the flowers of the field
When only a wind passes over them
They are gone
And the field forgets them

But your kindness
Stretches from forever to forever
Your rightness
Flows down through the generations
To those who keep faith with you
To those who walk your ways

You establish your throne in the center of things
Your kingdom embraces all
Blessings to you from the mighty angels
Who carry out the messages of your words
Blessings to you from the surrounding hosts
From the servants who build up your works
Blessings to you from all that you have made and are
In all the places throughout all the times—

My soul is for your blessing

My soul is for your blessing
For you are very great
Clothed with light and splendor
Wrapped in light like a garment
Who stretches out the sky like a curtain
Whose roof beams are fashioned with the waters
Whose chariots are the clouds
Who walks along the wind's wings
Whose messengers are the winds
Whose ministers are fire's flames
Who sets the earth upon her foundations
So that she cannot be moved
And covers her with waters like a robe
The waters stood high above the mountains
And with your blast they fled
Hearing your thunder they rushed away
Ascending the mountains
Pouring into the valleys
Until they found the place you'd set aside for them
Holding them within their borders
That they not return to engulf the earth
Who makes springs gush forth in the hills
So that between the hills brooks run clear
Giving drink to the roaming animals
There the deer come to slake their thirst
There the waterfowl nest
Sending out their voices
From between the nearby branches
You water the mountains from your lofts
Satisfy the earth with the fruits of your labor
Cause grasses to grow for the cattle
And herbs to respond to a human touch
So that people can bring forth crops from the land
And wine to gladden their hearts

And oil to make their faces glisten
And bread to sustain them
Full of sap are your trees
The cedars of Lebanon that you have planted
Where the birds make their nests
The heron has her home in the junipers
The high mountains are for wild goats
The cliffs a shelter for marmots
You made the moon for the seasons
Made the sun that knows when to set
You cause darkness to ripen into night
So that the night animals feel moved to stir
The young lions to roar for their prey
Asking you for their food
And when the sun comes up they return quietly home
To crouch asleep in their dens
Then people go out to do their work
And they labor until evening

How various are these deeds
That you have performed so shapely
The earth so full of your riches
Here is the vast wide sea
In which creatures without number
Of all sizes and kinds crawl and swim or drift and wave
There the great ships make their voyages
And huge whales journey and breach without tiring
All these wait upon you to give them their food in due
    season
What you give they gather
You open your hand and they are satisfied
Hide your face and they vanish
Remove your breath and they perish
Return to the dust they were made from

Breathe again your breath and they enter life renewed
Refreshing the face of the earth
Your glory endures forever
Your work is an endless rejoicing
You who glance at the earth and she trembles
Who touch the mountains and they smoke
While I live my songs will be for you
While I am I'll speak my gratefulness
May my words be agreeable
Yes I will share your rejoicing
May all that denies you be denied
And all that demeans you pass
My soul is for your blessing—
I praise that too

GRATITUDE TO YOU
In the goodness of your nature—
Your steadfast love never ends!

Thus the inspired ones speak
Those whom you redeemed from their suffering
Whom you gathered from the many lands
From the east and from the west
From the north and from the sea

They who wandered restless in the wilderness
In the desert pathways
And could not find a settled place
Hungry and thirsty, their souls grew faint

Then they cried out to you in their extremity
And you delivered them from their trials
Showing them a direct pathway
To a settled place

> Therefore they brim with thanks for your
>   steadfast love
> And praise your words to all humankind
> For you satisfy the longing soul
> And fill the hungry soul with goodness

And when they sat in the darkness of death's shadow
Miserably bound in those heavy irons
Because they had been heedless of your words
And ignorant of your counsel
You humbled their hearts with trouble
So that they stumbled and could find no help

Until they cried out to you in their extremity
And you saved them from their suffering
Bringing them out of the darkness of death's shadow
Tearing open their heavy bands

> Therefore they brim with thanks for your
>   steadfast love
> And praise your wonder to all humankind
> For you broke down the doors of copper
> Hacked open the bolts of iron

And for their heedless deeds
Their souls reject your sustenance
And they drift toward the shadow of death's gate

Until finally they cry to you in their extremity
And you save them from their suffering
Sending your healing words
You snatch them from their living graves

> And they brim with thanks for your steadfast
>   love
> And praise your wonder to all humankind
> And offer sacrifices of gratitude
> Singing your deeds with exalted notes

Those who go down to the sea in ships
Who do their work on the great waters
Know of your doings and wonders of the deep
You spoke and the storm winds stirred
Lifting up their terrible waves
That mounted up as far as heaven
And crashed down with the force of the bottomless deep

And their souls melted in their terror
And they reeled to and fro, staggering like drunks
And all their skill was useless

And they cried out to you in their extremity
And you brought them out of their suffering
Calmed the storm till it became a whisper
Tamed the sea's waves
And they rejoiced at the sudden stillness
And came back safely to port

> Brimming with thanks for your steadfast love
> And praising your wonders to all humankind
> Exalting you in the great congregations
> And in the assembly of elders

You changed river valleys into wastelands
And springs into parched ground
A fertile soil into a salt marsh
Because of the heedlessness of the people there
Changed the wasteland into a pool of clear water
And the desert into a spring
Invited the hungry to live there and find a settled place
To sow fields and plant vineyards
And enjoy the fruits of their labor
And blessed them and they increased
And their cattle remained robust
After for long they had not been robust
And were brought low by oppression misfortune and
        sorrow
Until you poured trouble over the heads of the powerful
And caused them to wander restless in the wilderness
In the desert pathways

And raised up the needy from their agony
And made their families plentiful as flocks

> The upright know this pattern and rejoice
> That the mouths of the heedless will be shut
>
> The wise observe this pattern
> And have confidence in your steadfast love

You whom I regularly praise
Do not ignore me now
For the crooked and deceitful
Are opening their mouths against me
Speaking of me everywhere with lying tongues
They have surrounded me with a cloud of hateful words
Have attacked me for no reason
Have repaid my kindness with accusations
And reduced me to nothing but this prayer
They repay my good with evil
Give me hatefulness in exchange for my love

Appoint someone harsh over him
With an accuser at his right hand
Let him be judged and convicted
And let his prayers turn sour in his mouth
Let his days be few
Let him know that someone else has taken his place
May his children be fatherless
His wife a widow
Let his children be continually restless
Begging for their keep in ruined places
Let his creditors put a lien on his property
And let strangers take their pick of his prized possessions
Let no one extend kindness to him
Or to his orphaned children
So that his seed will be cut off
And in another generation no one will know his name

Remember forever every sin his father's fathers ever
    committed
Let his mother's mothers' transgressions never be
    blotted out
Let all these misdoings be on your docket perpetually

So that any goodness they may have done has no chance
  of being remembered

Why all this?
Because he constantly remembered to be unkind
He persecuted the poor and needy
Those grieved in their hearts he rushed to destroy
He loved cursing—let it come back on him!
He hated blessing—let it be a million miles away!
May he wear cursing as his garment
May it enter into his body like water
Into his bones like oil
Let him wrap himself up in it like a cozy blanket
Let him hold up his pants with a cursing belt!
I ask you to give this for a reward to my accusers
To those who demean my soul for no good reason—

But you
O endless one—
Deal with me out of your better side
Kind as you are, save me
For I am poor and needy
And have a wounded heart
As the shadow fades at the close of day
So do I hasten away
As suddenly as locusts disappear
As abruptly will I be gone
My knees are knocking from my fasting
I am all skin and bones
When they see me they feel uneasy
And they shake their heads

Help me—out of your kindness save me
They will know that you have done it

They will see it is the work of your hand
Let them curse—you will bless
When they rise up in their haughtiness
Pull them down with shame
So that I can gloat
Let them be trussed up in their confusion
Wrapped up in their humiliation like a beggar's cloak

If you do this
I will compose thanksgiving songs to you
And I will travel far and wide singing them
For you are stationed at the right hand of the needy
To save him from people like that

Not for our sake, O Lord, not for us
But for the glory of your namelessness
For the sake of your kindness
For the sake of your truth

Why should the nations say
Where is their God?
When you abide hidden in things
And always accomplish what you intend
Their idols are silver and gold
The work of human hands
With mouths that do not speak
Eyes that do not see
Ears that do not hear
Noses that do not smell
They have hands that touch nothing
Feet that walk nowhere
Nor do they utter anything out of their throats
And those that made them
Are like them—everyone that trusted them

O strugglers!
Trust the imageless presence
          You who are our help and our shield
O house of Aaron, trust that
          It is our help and our shield
Fear it, trust it
          The only help, the final shield

You are constantly mindful of us
Bless us
Bless the strugglers
Bless Aaron's house
Bless those who fear you

The small together with the great
Who find increase more and more
For themselves and for their children
Who are blessed by the hand
That fashioned heaven and earth
Yours are the heavens
But the earth you give to the living
For the dead can't praise you
Those that have gone down to silence

But as for us—
We sing blessings to you from this day forth
Until a timeless and endless tomorrow

Nations, give praise
People, give praise
For strong is your steadfast love in us
And your truth is a durable truth
Without end—
Praise that

GRATITUDE TO YOU for your goodness
For your kindness pierces time through

Let those who struggle
Speak this
For your kindness pierces time through

Let the house of Aaron say this
For your kindness pierces time through

Let those whom you move with your power
Speak it out loud
For your kindness pierces time through

In my despair I called on you
And you answered me like the sky
You are for me—I cannot fear
For what can a man do to me?
You are for me—embrace me
And I can gaze with stillness at those who hate me

It is better to seek your shelter
Than to trust in people
It is better to seek your shelter
Than to trust in kings

Nations everywhere engulf me
But through your name I will surely cut them off

They encircle me all round,
Yes on all sides they surround me
But through your name I will surely cut them off

They buzz round me like bees
Blaze up like a thorn fire
But through your name I will surely cut them off

They thrust at me murderously
But you protect me

You are my strength and my song
My rescue

The voice of rejoicing and comfort rings through the
    tents of the upright
And your right hand upholds it
Exalts it
Your right hand upholds

I will not die I will live
To speak of what you do
You who have laid me low for my errors
But have never given me up

Open for me the gates of uprightness
I will enter them and give thanks
This is the gate that belongs to you
The gate the upright enter

I give thanks to you for you have answered me
Become my rescue

The stone that the builders rejected
Is now become the cornerstone
Because of you
And it is miraculous to our eyes

This is the day you have made
In it we will be glad and rejoice
And we pray: Send us happiness

Blessed is the one who comes in your name
Whom we bless out of your house
You are our sovereign, our light

Bind the festival offering with cord
Bring it to the horns of the altar

For you are my sovereign and I give thanks to you
You I exalt and praise

Accept my gratitude
Throughout your goodness

For your kindness pierces time through

I LIFT MY EYES to the mountain peak—
Where does my help come from?
It comes from you
Maker of heaven and earth
Who holds my foot firm on the path up
Who's constantly present
Everywhere aware

Look!
With you there's no obscurity
Nothing is dim, asleep, inert
To those who question and struggle
You respond, keep hold, give cover
So that by day the sun won't burn
Nor by night the moon mesmerize

You guard against evil
Enfold and reveal the soul

Guard my arrival
Secure my departure—
Now:

Always

JOY DRENCHED ME when you said
Come inside my house
Now our feet stand within your gates, Jerusalem
Planted upon your wholeness

Jerusalem,
Place where each is welcome
All belong

For this is the place
Toward which people ascend
Giving thanks with their mouths
Singing the thousand names of the nameless
And here stand the upright chairs of David's justice

Pray for the peace of Jerusalem
Pray that all who love her will be well
May there be peace within her walls
Plenty in her palaces

For the sake of all that lives and is
Let me speak these heart words:
Peace, peace,
Peace for Jerusalem

And for your sake
From inside your house
I pledge myself to seek the good

UP TOWARD YOU
I lift my eyes:
Look!
As manservants raise eyes toward masters
As maidservants raise eyes toward mistresses
Humble and expectant
In reflected gratefulness
So do we direct our gaze
Up to you

Reflect in our souls your clear light
Enlarge our hearts

For we are diminished and dimmed with the world's
    opinions
Diminished and dimmed with possession and worry
With accomplishment's undertow
With reputation's crazy wind
Oppressed by the disdaining other
Inside and out

IF YOU HAD NOT STOOD BY US
We who rise to question and struggle
We would have said: If you had not stood by us
When the world's weight fell we are broken
When the world's flood surged we are swept down
Souls sunk in a watery cell
Breath cut off
The torrents washing out our dispersal
The presumptuous waters
Rolling down the nothing
The zero that remains

So we speak the unsayable name
Blessing you who have held us whole
Kept us from all that is trapped partial and torn

Because of you
Our soul flutters light
Like a bird escaped from a fowler's snare
The snare is snapped and we fly up

Our help is in your unnameable name
Word of all words inside the ear
You to whom all speech is addressed

LIKE UNMOVABLE ZION
Which endures, patient and firm
Are those who trust in you
Whose speech is your unsayableness
Whose heart your unknowable love

**Psalm
125**

Jerusalem is ringed with peaks
As you ring in us now
Our impassable reverberating frontier

For the territory of the crooked the cruel and the mute
Does not border on the open lands of the upright

This place is self- and all-connected, sole
And cannot touch what it is not

So you bring goodness to goodness
Uprightness to uprightness
But the crooked and heedless
Will continue uneven
In endless agitation
Even as we who question and struggle
Find a towering lasting and patient peace

WHEN YOU BRING US OUT from enclosure
We will be like dreamers
Our heads thrown back with laughter
Our throats vibrating with song
And the others will say

Yes
Great happenings
Have happened to them
The ones who have struggled
Long with their questions

Yes
Great things would have happened to us
And we would be dizzy with the joy of them
Drunk on water in an arid land
Our tears our joy's seed
We'd go out weeping
And come back singing
Our arms full of sheaves

Happy is the one who stands in awe of you
Who walks your pathways

When he eats what his hands have harvested
He is content and all is well
His wife is like a fruitful vine beside the house
His children like olive saplings round about the table

Who stands in awe of you is happy
Knows your blessing in Zion
Sees Jerusalem's joy a whole life long
And lives to see grandchildren—

May there be peace one day
For all who question and struggle

OUT OF THE DEPTHS I call to you
Listen to my voice
Be attentive to my supplicating voice

If you tallied errors
Who would survive the count?
But you forgive, you forbear everything
And this is the wonder and the dread

You are my heart's hope, my daily hope
And my ears long to hear your words
My heart waits quiet in hope for you
More than they who watch for sunrise
Hope for a new morning

Let those who question and struggle
Wait quiet like this for you
For with you there is durable kindness
And wholeness in abundance
And you will loose all our bindings
Surely

You KNOW THAT MY HEART is not haughty
Nor my eyes lofty
Neither have I reached for things
Too great and too wonderful for me

But I have calmed and settled my heart
And it is contented

Like a child surfeited on a mother's breast
Like a suckling child is my heart

Let those who question and struggle
Wait quiet like this for you
From this day forth
And always

How GOOD
How pleasant
When we abide intimate together
Like warm oil on the head
Trickling down the cheek
Aaron's cheek
And trickling down the neck onto the collar
Like the dew of Mount Hermon
The dew that runs down the mountains of Zion
Where you called forth the blessing
For life, life always

WE SAT BY THE WATERS of Babylon
And wept when we remembered Zion
Upon the bending willows there we hung our harps
For in our exile we were forced to utter words of
    home—
Sing for us the songs of Zion
But it was mockery
How could we sing our songs on strangers' soil?

If I forget you Jerusalem
Let my right hand forget its cunning
Let my tongue lock my mouth mute
If I forget to turn back to you
If I lose my way and wander off from you Jerusalem
Source of my heart's comfort

Reward justly all that weakens her
All that longs to see her uprooted and wiped away

O daughters of Babylon!
In your actions are the seeds of your fall
And it will be a relief to see those seeds bear fruit
For what you have done
A relief when your dark sprouts and black flowers
Are dashed against the rock of faith

**Psalm
137**

You have searched me inside and out with your beam **Psalm**
You have known me **139**
You know my sitting down and my rising up
You think my thoughts before they arrive in my mind
You are my walking
You are my lying down
All my living is your knowing

Even before there's a word on my tongue you speak it
You're behind me and before me
Your hand touches me wherever I am
And my knowing this is impossible for it is
    indecipherably sweet
Too exalted for my heart to grasp: inconceivable

Where could I go to be apart from you?
To what place flee from your presence?
If I should ascend to heaven you're there
And if I am cast down to the bottom world you're there
    too
If I should fly up with the wings of the morning
If I should dwell in the depths of the sea
Even there I'd feel your touch, your grip

If I said, I'll pull up the darkness
Cover all the world's light with the dark
Even that darkness wouldn't be dark
But would be bright as clear noon
Because in you darkness and light are one

You guided me into this world
Placed me in the waters of my mother's womb
And I am grateful to be so wonderfully, so terribly,
    made

Awesome is what is, what you are!
And this I know in the secret silences of my heart
Where your awareness dwells
And embroiders me into the fabric of the physical
    world
Out of the slender thread only your eyes can see
Recorded by your hand into the book of the world
All the days of my recordable life
Even before I live them

How inconceivably precious are your thoughts!
And the sum of them—how great!
In my dreams I count them
And they are more numerous than sands
And I awake, still with you
To make this passionate request:

Zero out the crooked
Let the destroyers be absent
Those who mistake the love for you
Twisting it in their selfishness—
Those that despise you I will also despise

When they rise against you I will feel horror
And I will hate them with the utmost hatred
And though they be as myself I will make enemies of
    them

Search me inside and out with your beam
Pour your awareness throughout my heart like honey
And find the crookedness and selfishness there
And lead me away from it
On the way to your timeless time

Blessings on you, my rock
Who strengthens my hand for the fight
My fingers for the fray
You are my kindness and my fortress
My castle, my rescue, my shield
Whom I most trust
Who orders my impulses

What am I that you recognize me?
And my children, that you recognize them?
I am a breath
My days like a passing shadow

Bend the sky down till it fills the earth!
Caress the mountains till they burst into flames!
Scatter lightning till they run frightened away
Shoot out thunderbolts and terrify them
Stretch out your sky hands
And pluck me from these turbulent waters
From the grip of the children of the stranger
Whose mouth speaks seductions
And whose right hand is the hand of the lie

A new song will I sing for you
On the ten-stringed psaltery will I pluck my praises

You give victory to kings, rid David your servant
Of the bloodthirsty sword, so rid me
And rescue me from the grip of the children of the
     stranger
Whose mouth speaks seductions
And whose right hand is the hand of the lie
So that my sons may be like vigorous plants
And my daughters like the palace cornerstones

May the granaries be full with many grains
The sheep crowd the open pastures in the thousands
Tens of thousands, may the oxen be strong
And may there be no breaking in or breaking out
Or shouting in the streets

Happy are they who live like this
Happy those who give themselves to you

I WILL HOLD YOU HIGHEST in my heart
Will pronounce with blessing your unsayable name
Everywhere and always

Each of my days will be a blessing for you
And I will sing your unsayableness
Everywhere and always

You are large and largely to be embraced
Your greatness is unsearchable
Generation after generation shall praise your works
And they shall name and recount your powerful acts

I will stop
And consider
Your burning beauty
Your wondrous deeds
I will stop and speak
Of your awesome acts
I will stop and remember
Your greatness

People will proclaim memorials to your goodness
They will sing full-throated of your rightness

For you are gracious and compassionate
Long-suffering and overflowing with kindness
Good to all, and your tender mercies wash the world clean
So that everything is drenched in gratefulness
And those who love you bless you with every breath
And converse always of the brightness of your presence
Speak only of your power and pervasiveness
To make clear to the onrushing generations

That your acts are decisive
Your presence is bright
Your rule is timeless
And your pattern weaves through all that is

You hold up the falling ones
You lift up those who are pressed down
All eyes wait upon you hopefully
And when it is time you give them what they need
Opening your hand to satisfy them

Your rightness gleams in all action
Your goodness seeps into every hidden place
For those who call you in their heart's truth
You are there in the calling
And you fulfill all those who embrace your power
You hear their cries and they are saved

In your love you preserve those who love you
But in your distance you are the abandonment of those
    who abandon you

My mouth shall ever speak these words of praise for you
And all flesh shall be the blessing of your unsayable name
Everywhere and always

MY SOUL BRIMS WITH gratitude for you
Whom I'll praise all my life—
As long as I am I'll sing your songs

Don't put your trust in the powerful
Mere people who can hold but never save
When their breath leaves them
They return to the earth they're made of
And on that day
All their hopes end

But happy is the one
Who trusts you for help
Whose hope rests with you

Who made the heavens, the earth, the sea, and all it
    holds
Whose truth is endless
Who brings justice to the oppressed
Bread to the hungry
Who frees the bound
Teaches the blind to see
Lifts up the bent over
Who loves the upright
Guards the stranger
Protects the orphan and widow
And provides the heedless with the trouble they need

You whose way is right forever
Zion's guide for all the generations—
Praise is yours

PRAISE:
How good it is to sing to you
How pleasant to chant these songs

You build up Jerusalem
All the dispersed strugglers you bring home
You heal their broken hearts, soothe their wounds
You count all the stars in the sky leaving none out
And call them each by name

This is how great you are
This is how endless your power is
How immeasurable your wisdom is

You lift up the bent over
But the heedless you bring back down to earth

So we raise up this song to you with gratefulness
Singing your praises with the harp's strings
Who covers the heavens with floating clouds
And loosens rain for the thirsty earth
And makes grass grow green on the mountains
And feeds the young ravens when they impatiently caw

Who doesn't delight in the brute power of the horse
Or in the swiftness of men's legs
But takes pleasure in the selfless loving
Of those who wait gently for your love

So let Jerusalem glorify you
Let Zion be only for your praise
Who makes the bars of her gates strong
And blesses her children

And pacifies her borders
And satisfies the people with choice wheat

You send forth your healing word
Out over the earth
Swiftly speeding it along
In the snow you sprinkle like chilly fleece
In the frost you scatter like icy ashes
In the hail you hurl like frozen diamonds—
Who can stand your cold?
You send out your words
And it all melts
Your warm breath blows and the waters surge

You send your commands to the one who wrestles with
     you
Your ordinances to those who question and struggle
And to no one else
The others do not know of them—
For this too we are grateful

PRAISE TO YOU from the sky's boundary
Praise to you from the mountain's crown
Praise to you from winged angels
From all the hosts of heaven and earth
The stars and their unimaginable brightness
The heavens in their silent dome
And the waters beyond those heavens
All wordlessly praise your unnameable name
For by your timeless speech
All is created—why should it be?
And all is established endlessly
Your unsayable saying that none can unsay
All life of earth is your praise
And the life of the sea and all unknowable depths
Fire and hail, snow and cloud
Tornado and hurricane—all is your speaking
Mountains and hills, fruit trees and cedars
Wildcats, cattle, buzzards, birds
Kings and their subjects, princes, judges
Young men, young women, old men, boys—
All are your name's praising
For your unspeakableness alone is what is
Your brightness lights the earth and sky
Raises us up, blares out the note
From your people's trumpet
An exultant blast for all who struggle with you
And are close at hand

Psalm 148

PRAISE TO YOU in your holiness
Praise throughout your expansive realm
Praise for the power of your doing
For your abundance and everywhereness
All praise
Praise with the blowing of trumpets
Praise with the psaltery and harp
Praise with timbrel and dance
With stringed instrument and pipe
Praise with clear-sounding cymbals
And with crashing cymbals

Every breath is your praise

**Psalm
150**

A NOTE ON SOURCES AND STYLE

The main source I have used for these versions of the Psalms is a small Hebrew-English text I picked up in Israel, *Sefer Tehilim—The Book of Psalms, Hebrew-English*. It was published in 1993 by Sinai Publishing, in Tel-Aviv, and, oddly, no translator or editor is listed. I also relied on the English version of the Psalms in the Tanach of the Jewish Publication Society, as well as the King James Version, which is in many important ways quite different. Additionally, I looked at various translations of selected Psalms that appear in Jewish prayer books, as well as numerous renderings of the Psalms into English by poets and translators, both contemporary and from the seventeenth through the nineteenth centuries. I read various scholarly papers that my Catholic friends were kind enough to give me, and I consulted the brief commentaries given for each psalm in the Jerome Bible, a Catholic scholarly source.

Stylistically, I follow the verse format I most often use in my own poems, each line beginning with a capital letter and no periods at the end of sentences. To indicate pauses or conclusions to a particular thought I use stanza breaks or dashes.

Made in the USA
Lexington, KY
23 May 2011